MACMILLAN ACADEMIC SKILLS

C000139643

Skillful
Reading&Writing

Student's Book

1

Author: David Bohlke
Series Consultant: Dorothy E. Zemach

Contents

Contents

Vocabulary skill	Grammar	Writing skill	Writing task	Digibook video activity	Study skills
Using examples to find meaning	The simple present tense	Writing topic sentences	Describing a hero	What makes a hero?	Setting up a study space
Organizing new words: nouns and verbs	Verbs followed by infinitives and gerunds	Understanding sentence patterns	Describing how to achieve a goal	Time flies as you get older	Writing for the fearful
Using explanations to find meaning	*There is / are* (+ quantifier) + noun	Brainstorming word maps	Describing your home	How our homes have changed	Reviewing and practicing vocabulary
Using definitions to find meaning	The present progressive tense	Writing compound sentences	Describing how your neighborhood is changing	Reaching for the skies	Process writing
Adding prefixes for negation	Giving advice and making suggestions	Using end punctuation and capitalization	Giving advice in an email	Spots and stripes	Where does the time go?
Organizing new words: adjectives and adverbs	Comparative forms of adjectives and adverbs	Using commas and colons	Making a comparison	A need for speed	Keeping a journal
Adding suffixes to change verbs into nouns	Count and noncount nouns	Writing complete sentences	Describing colors	Learning to see	Studying with others
Understanding compound words	Expressing ability	Using transitions to add and emphasize information	Giving your opinion	Pushing the limits	Using computers for effective study
Finding the correct definition of a word	The simple past tense	Using transitions to sequence events	Describing a memorable day	Saving the bees	Making the most of your dictionary
Using collocations	Future forms	Using parallel structure	Describing your future	Work and motivation	Making the most of the library

To the Student

Academic success requires so much more than memorizing facts. It takes skills. This means that a successful student can both learn and think critically.

Skillful gives you:

- Skills for learning about a wide variety of topics from different angles and from different academic areas
- Skills you need to succeed when reading and listening to these texts
- Skills you need to succeed when writing for and speaking to different audiences
- Skills for critically examining the issues presented by a speaker or a writer
- Study skills for learning and remembering the English language and important information.

To successfully use this book, use these strategies:

- Come to class prepared to learn. This means that you should show up well-fed, well-rested, and prepared with the proper materials (paper, pen, textbook, completed homework, and so on).
- Ask questions and interact. Learning a language is not passive. You need to actively participate. Help your classmates, and let them help you. It is easier to learn a language with other people.
- Practice! Do each exercise a few times, with different partners. Memorize and use new language. Use the *Skillful* Digibook to develop the skills presented in the Student's Book. Complete the additional activities on your computer outside of class to make even more progress.
- Review your work. Look over the skills, grammar, and vocabulary from previous units. Study a little bit each day, not just before tests.
- Be an independent learner, too. Look for opportunities to study and practice English outside of class, such as reading for pleasure and using the Internet in English. Find and then share information about the different unit topics with your classmates.

Remember that learning skills, like learning a language, takes time and practice. Be patient with yourself, but do not forget to set goals. Check your progress and be proud of your success!

I hope you enjoy using *Skillful*!

Dorothy E. Zemach
Series Consultant

Welcome to *Skillful*!

Each *Skillful* unit has ten pages and is divided into two main sections: reading skills and writing skills.

Reading

The reading skills section always comes first and starts with a *Discussion point* to lead you in to the unit topic.

There are then two reading texts for you to practice your reading skills on. There are activities to practice your global reading skills and your close reading skills, as well as opportunities to critically examine the ideas in the texts. Key academic vocabulary from the text is presented on the page so you can see essential terms to learn.

Vocabulary skills also give you the chance to develop the ways in which you learn and remember vocabulary from the reading texts.

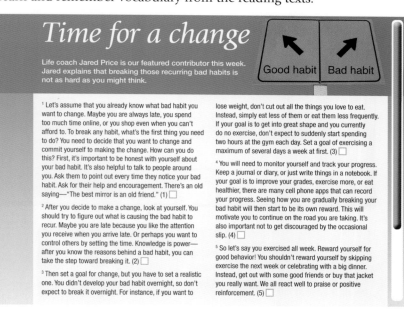

Writing

The writing section has two main parts: grammar and writing skills. You can find information on each of these in boxes on the page and these give essential information on these skills. At the end of this section is a writing task for you to put the ideas from the texts and the skills from the writing section into practice. Use the checklist on page 109 to see how well your partner has completed the task.

The final page in the unit focuses on study skills which will help you to achieve academic success. Some of these pages come from *The Study Skills Handbook* by Stella Cottrell, while others are engaging scenarios for you to read and reflect on.

Using *Skillful* gives you everything you need for academic success.

Good luck!

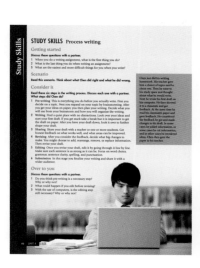

Introduction

Each *Skillful* Student's Book comes with a code in the back of the book that gives you free access to the accompanying Digibook. The Digibook encourages a more interactive and engaging learning environment and is very simple to access. Just go to www.skillfuldigibooks.com, and follow the step-by-step instructions to get started!

The first time you access the Digibook you will need an Internet connection, but after this it is possible to work offline if you wish.

Digital Student's Book

This contains all the same content as your printed Student's Book, but you can use it on your computer, enabling easier navigation through the pages, a zoom function to create better student focus, and a personal annotation resource for helpful classroom notes.

Skillful Practice

You can either complete the extra activities as you go through the Digital Student's Book via the interactive icons, or you can find them all in one place in the *Skillful* Practice area. Here you will find a variety of activities to practice all the new skills and language you have learned in the Student's Book, including vocabulary, grammar and skills-based activities.

There are also additional productive tasks and video activities linked to the unit topics.

If you complete any of the extra activities while you are online, your score will be recorded in your markbook so that your teacher can track your progress. If you work offline your scores will be stored and transferred to your markbook the next time you connect.

Whether online or offline, in the classroom or on the move, the *Skillful* Digibook allows you to access and use its content while encouraging interactive learning and effortless self-study.

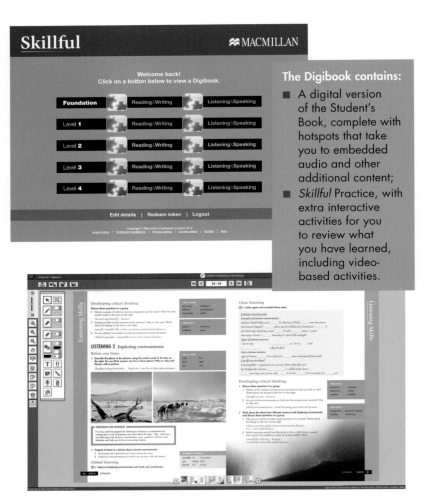

The Digibook contains:

- A digital version of the Student's Book, complete with hotspots that take you to embedded audio and other additional content;
- *Skillful* Practice, with extra interactive activities for you to review what you have learned, including video-based activities.

The Digital Student's Book also contains lots of hotspots that link to additional content not in your printed Student's Book:

- Audio files for all of the reading texts
- Useful language to support discussion activities
- Dictionary definitions for the *Academic Keywords*
- Unit checklists so you can monitor how well you are progressing through the course.

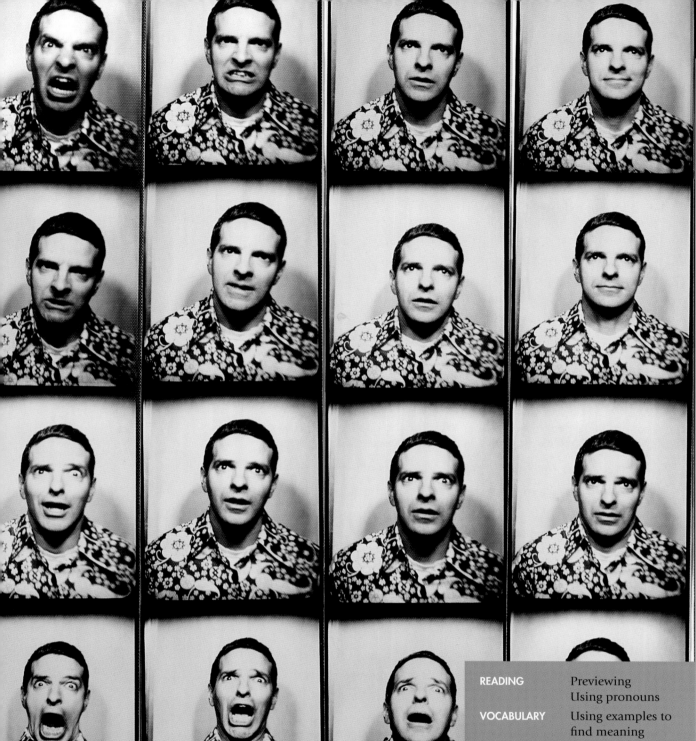

READING	Previewing
	Using pronouns
VOCABULARY	Using examples to find meaning
WRITING	Writing topic sentences
GRAMMAR	The simple present tense

Discussion point

Discuss these questions with a partner.

1 How would you describe the personality of the man in the picture?

I would describe his personality as ...

2 How would you describe your personality? Do you think others would describe you in the same way?

I think I'm ... . Others would probably describe me as ...

3 What superheroes do you know? What personality traits do they have? Are they all positive traits?

Batman is ... . They are positive / negative traits.

Vocabulary preview

Read these sentences. In each set of five, match the words in bold with their meanings.

1 If you can, try to **contribute** something to charity. ___   **a** truthful
2 How do you **cope with** stress in your life? ___   **b** who someone is
3 My parents taught me to be **honest** and never lie. ___   **c** not win
4 Let children develop their own sense of **identity**. ___   **d** give
5 I do not want to **lose** the spelling contest. ___   **e** handle

6 Teachers have clear learning **objectives** in mind. ___   **f** without faults
7 No one is **perfect**. We all make mistakes. ___   **g** value
8 My parents **respect** hard work. ___   **h** achieve something
9 If you work hard, you will **succeed**. ___   **i** lack of strength
10 Do not show your **weakness** in a business meeting. ___   **j** goals

READING 1   Are you a natural leader?

Before you read

1 **What are these people known for? Which of the qualities in the box on the right do you think they have in common? Discuss with a partner.**

... is known for ... . These people might all have ... in common, because ...

> **PREVIEWING**
>
> When you preview a text, you look quickly at the title, headings, photos, and captions before reading the text. This gives you a sense of its structure, content, and how much time you will need to read it.

2 **Preview *Are you a natural leader?* Discuss these questions.**
What kind of text is it? What will you probably do with the text?

Global reading

Read *Are you a natural leader?* quickly. Was your preview correct?

Close reading

1 **Read *Are you a natural leader?* Check (✓) the statements that are true for you. Do you agree with what it says about you?**

2 **Match these statements with statements in *Are you a natural leader?* Write the number.**

a "I try to fix problems." ___
b "I can do more than one thing at once." ___
c "I enjoy new experiences." ___
d "I know what I'm not good at." ___
e "I enjoy being around a lot of people." ___
f "I never lie." ___

QUALITIES

calmness	happiness
confidence	intelligence
friendliness	kindness

Martin Luther King, Jr.   Hilary Clinton

Ban Ki-moon

Marie Curie

Mark Zuckerberg   J.K. Rowling

3 **Read these statements. Find statements in *Are you a natural leader?* that mean the opposite. Write the number.**

a "It's important to win, win, win!" ____

b "Sometimes I'm a little disorganized." ____

c "I can't say what I think very clearly." ____

d "I always get nervous when I talk in front of others." ____

e "I'm uncomfortable about some things I decide." ____

f "I prefer people just to listen when we're in a discussion." ____

ACADEMIC KEYWORDS		
decision	(n)	/dɪˈsɪʒ(ə)n/
describe	(v)	/dɪˈskraɪb/
stress	(n)	/stres/

Practical Psychology *magazine asks,*

"ARE YOU A NATURAL LEADER?"

Take our personality survey and find out. The results may surprise you.

1 I like to try new things.
2 I'm a very organized person.
3 I like to be in charge during a project.
4 People respect my ideas.
5 I like to push myself.
6 I bring out the best in others.
7 I state my ideas clearly.
8 I'm not perfect and am aware of my weaknesses.
9 I'm confident of my public speaking skills.
10 Clear objectives are important to me.
11 I'm comfortable with my decisions.
12 If there's a problem, I try to solve it.
13 I want everyone to contribute in discussions.
14 People describe me as a "people person."

15 Change doesn't bother me.
16 I cope with stress well.
17 I'm able to do several things at the same time.
18 It's important for me to be honest.
19 I want the people around me to succeed.
20 I feel it's sometimes OK to lose.

SURVEY RESULTS

11–20 points You are definitely a natural leader. You will make it big in this world.

6–10 points You have some traits of a natural leader.

0–5 points You are not a natural leader. But you can still develop into a strong leader.

Developing critical thinking

Discuss these questions in a group.

1 Can you name any natural leaders? Do the sentences in the text describe them?

I think ... is a natural leader. The sentences in the text do / don't describe him / her because ...

2 What other characteristics do you think natural leaders have?

I think natural leaders also have ...

3 What is the worst fault a leader can have? Think about the faults in the box on the right.

The worst fault a leader can have is ... because ...

FAULTS	
anger	dishonesty
arrogance	stupidity

READING 2 The hero within

Before you read

1 Do you ever read comic books or watch movies or TV shows about superheroes? Why or why not? Discuss with a partner.

I often / sometimes / never read comic books about superheroes because ...

2 Preview *The hero within*. What is it about?

Global reading

Read *The hero within*. <u>Underline</u> the seven things that make a superhero.

Close reading

1 Complete these sentences. Use no more than three words for each answer.

1 Superheroes are enjoying a _____.

2 In some cases, friends or family know a superhero's _____, but it's usually a secret.

3 Because of the superhero's _____, he or she rarely kills.

4 Superheroes and super-villains symbolize the opposite ideas of _____.

5 A superhero would be very _____ without a weakness.

6 Superhero stories speak important truths about _____.

7 Two examples of what a superhero's enemies may symbolize are _____ and _____.

8 A superhero is a true hero because he or she is not _____.

USING PRONOUNS

A pronoun is a word that replaces a noun. We use pronouns to avoid repeating the noun. It must always be clear what a pronoun refers to. This is called the pronoun's antecedent.

One common error with pronouns is when there is no antecedent.

*In the restaurant, **they** said I had to leave.* (Who said I had to leave?)

Another common error is when the antecedent is ambiguous.

*Maria told Lynn that **her** purse was missing.*
(Is Maria's purse or Lynn's purse missing?)

---

2 Read these sentences from *The hero within*. Write the words the pronouns in bold refer to.

1 All superheroes are honest and possess a strong moral code. **They** respect the law but will break **it** if doing so will contribute to the greater good.

   a They = _____   **b** it = _____

2 A weakness can make a superhero helpless. **This** is also what makes **him or her** interesting.

   a This = _____   **b** him or her = _____

3 And the superhero's enemies are our own fears, such as crime and war. **They** receive names and faces so that our superhero can face **them**.

   a They = _____   **b** them = _____

THE HERO WITHIN

[1] Batman, Jubilee, the X-Men—all are superheroes. We find them in comic books, movies, novels, toys, and video games all over the world. Superheroes were part of Western culture for much of the 20th century, and they are currently enjoying a rebirth in this century. What makes a superhero, and why are they likely not going anywhere soon? Let's look at seven things that superheroes share.

1 [2] Nearly all fictional superheroes have super-human powers. For example, Superman can fly and Wonder Woman can talk with animals. Some add to their powers with technology, such as Iron Man's metal suit or the Green Lantern's ring.

2 [3] A secret identity helps protect the superhero's family and friends. In a few cases friends and family know the superhero's identity—that Spider-Man is really Peter Parker or that Bruce Banner is actually the Hulk. Some superheroes also have secret headquarters, like Batman's Batcave.

3 [4] A colorful costume, such as Spider-Man's web design or Captain America's U.S. flag costume, helps the public recognize the superhero, and at the same time it hides his or her identity. Some costumes also have an emblem, such as Superman's *S* or the *4* for members of the Fantastic Four.

4 [5] All superheroes are honest and possess a strong moral code. They respect the law but will break it if doing so will contribute to the greater good. Superheroes expect no reward and rarely kill.

5 [6] Superheroes would not exist without the super-villain. Superheroes and super-villains often have similar powers, but one uses the power for good and the other for evil.

6 [7] As a child Bruce Wayne saw a man kill his parents. He coped with this tragedy by training and later becoming Batman. The backstory tells how the superhero actually became the superhero we know. Superheroes are rarely born that way.

7 [8] A weakness can make a superhero helpless. This is also what makes him or her interesting. Superman has no power against the mineral Kryptonite, Wolverine dislikes magnets, and the Hulk's own anger is his worst enemy. To succeed they must overcome this weakness.

[9] The superhero is perhaps not so different from us. It is the purpose of the story that speaks to us. They tell important truths about human nature. Perhaps there is a superhero inside all of us? The superhero is an ideal, a symbol of our hopes, goals, and objectives. These are qualities that we see in ourselves—our inner hero. And the superhero's enemies are our own fears, such as crime and war. They receive names and faces so that our superhero can face them. The superhero often loses but never, ever quits. This is a lesson we can all learn from. Like us, the superhero is not perfect, but that's exactly what makes a true hero.

ACADEMIC KEYWORDS		
code	(n)	/koʊd/
overcome	(v)	/ˌoʊvərˈkʌm/
possess	(v)	/pəˈzes/

Developing critical thinking

1 Discuss these questions in a group.

1 Why are superhero comics, movies, and video games so popular?

I think they're popular because ...

2 Do you agree with the article's definition? How would you define a superhero?

I do / don't agree. I would define a superhero as ...

2 Think about the ideas from *Are you a natural leader?* and *The hero within* and discuss these questions in a group.

1 Can an everyday hero be a superhero? Think about the things in the box on the right.

I believe that an everyday hero can / can't be a superhero because ...

2 Do you think superheroes are natural leaders? Why or why not?

In my opinion, superheroes are / aren't natural leaders because ...

THINK ABOUT:	
intelligence	strength
money	villains
powers	weakness

Vocabulary skill

USING EXAMPLES TO FIND MEANING

When you find a new word, context clues such as examples help you discover the word's meaning. Sometimes the text will give an example that helps you to understand a word's meaning.

Words that signal examples: *for example, for instance, such as, like*

1 Read these sentences from *The hero within*. Circle the correct meaning of the words in bold.

1 Nearly all fictional superheroes have **super-human** powers. For example, Superman can fly and Wonder Woman can talk with animals.

    a something all humans have

    b beyond what humans have

2 Some superheroes also have secret **headquarters**, like Batman's Batcave.

    a the leader of an organization

    b administrative center of an organization

3 Some costumes also have an **emblem**, such as Superman's *S* or the 4 for members of the Fantastic Four.

    a a sign that represents something else

    b any costume decoration

2 Read these sentences about superheroes. Circle the correct meaning of the words in bold.

1 There have been several **sequels** to the original 1989 Batman film, such as *Batman Returns*, *Batman and Robin*, and *The Dark Knight Rises*.

    a movies that continue a previous story

    b movies that are better than the original

2 Sometimes a superhero's senses are **enhanced**. For instance, a superhero may be able to hear noise from a great distance.

    a weakened

    b strengthened

3 Superheroes are popular in several **genres**, like comic books and movies.

    a things that young people enjoy

    b literary categories

WRITING Describing a hero

You are going to learn about writing topic sentences and using the simple present tense. You are then going to use these to write a paragraph describing a person you think is a hero.

Writing skill

WRITING TOPIC SENTENCES

A paragraph is a sequence of sentences that work together to support one main idea. This main idea is expressed in a topic sentence. All the sentences in a paragraph should support the main idea of the topic sentence. A topic sentence is *not* a title or a statement of what you are going to write about. It usually comes at or near the beginning of a paragraph.

1 Read these statements about topic sentences. Write *T* (True) or *F* (False).

1 A paragraph consists of sentences that support one idea.

2 Several ideas are expressed in a topic sentence.

3 The sentences in a paragraph need to support the topic sentence.

4 A topic sentence is the same thing as the title of a paragraph.

5 A topic sentence is always at or near the beginning of a paragraph.

2 Look back at the *The hero within*. Underline the topic sentence in each paragraph.

3 Circle the best topic sentence for each topic.

Topic 1: Heroes
a My heroes
b All heroes have five important qualities.
c I will write about what a hero means to me.

Topic 2: Personality tests
a Online personality tests
b Most personality tests are unreliable.
c The best place to find personality tests

Topic 3: How to build character
a This paragraph discusses character building.
b Building character is not only the job of teachers.
c The definition of "character"

4 Write two possible topic sentences for these topics.

Topic 1: Superhero movies
Topic 2: My personality
Topic 3: Everyday heroes

Grammar

THE SIMPLE PRESENT TENSE

The simple present tense is used to describe facts or general truths, and actions that are usual or repeated. These actions can be a hobby, a daily event, or a scheduled event. Study the forms:

Form	Example
Affirmative *I / You / We / They* + base form *He / She / It* + base form + *-s*	I agree. She agrees.
Negative *I / You / We / They* + *do not* + base form *He / She / It* + *does not* + base form	I do not agree. She does not agree.

Verbs often used in the simple present tense: *believe, belong, feel, hate, hear, know, like, love, mean, prefer, remain, realize, see, seem, think, understand, want*

Irregular verbs: *have / has, do / does,* and *go / goes.*

1 Complete these sentences. Use the simple present tense of the verbs in the box.

belong   have   know   like   see   think

1 I _____ superhero stories are just for kids.
2 My brother _____ a lot of comic books.
3 My friends and I _____ the X-Men.
4 I _____ the plots of most superhero stories.
5 Our teachers _____ hero qualities in us.
6 These comic books _____ to my cousin.

2 Rewrite the sentences in exercise 1 in the negative.

WRITING TASK

Read this paragraph. <u>Underline</u> the topic sentence. ⟨Circle⟩ the verbs in the simple present tense.

Everyone has a hero. I think that everyday heroes like police officers and firefighters are true heroes. My hero is my Uncle Manuel. He works as a police officer. I really respect him. He protects our city and keeps us safe. He works long and difficult hours. For example, he often works from 11:00 p.m. to 7:00 a.m. He has to cope with a stressful and difficult job, but he never complains. He is a very honest man. He does not make much money. He does this work because he cares about people. He wants to help them and contribute something to our city. People sometimes thank him. I want more people to do that. We need to appreciate these everyday heroes more.

BRAINSTORM

Who is *your* everyday hero? Why? Complete the word map with your ideas.

My hero

PLAN

Plan a paragraph describing your hero. Look back at your brainstorm and write a topic sentence. Include at least three reasons.

WRITE

Write your paragraph. Pay attention to your use of the present simple tense.

SHARE

Exchange paragraphs with a partner. Look at the checklist on page 109 and provide feedback to your partner.

REWRITE AND EDIT

Consider your partner's comments and rewrite your paragraph.

STUDY SKILLS Setting up a study space

Getting started

Discuss these questions with a partner.

1 Where do you usually study? Do you always study in the same place?
2 Do you prefer to study in a quiet place or a place with some background noise?
3 What is a study space? Why do you think creating a study space is important for many people?

Scenario

Read this scenario. Think about what Hamid is doing right and what he is doing wrong.

Hamid lives at home with his parents and brother. He is a civil engineering student in his first year at university. He has created a space in his bedroom where he does most of his studying. He has a small desk that faces a bare wall. On the desk he has a computer and a large workspace where he can spread out his books and papers. Hamid sometimes lies on his bed when he studies, especially when he wants to watch something on TV. He shares the bedroom with his little brother. Hamid gets annoyed because sometimes his brother comes into their room and makes noise.

Consider it

Read these seven tips for how to set up a study space. Discuss each one with a partner. Are all of them important for effective studying?

1 **Claim your space** Decide where you work best and use that space for studying, and only studying.
2 **Get comfortable** Set up your chair, desk, and computer so they do not harm your neck, back, or wrists.
3 **Stock it** Have everything you need nearby, such as pens, an eraser, dictionaries, a thesaurus, notebooks, and your printer. Keep everything neat and organized.
4 **Spread out** Make sure you have enough space to spread out your books, papers, and anything else you are using.
5 **Turn it off** Turn off the TV, your phone, and instant messaging. They will just distract you.
6 **Set rules** Establish rules about your study space and share them. These can include things like study hours, and when and how you can be interrupted.
7 **Personalize it** You will spend a lot of time in your study space, so enjoy it. Add posters, notes, and photos. They may just inspire you!

Over to you

Discuss these questions with a partner.

1 Which of the tips apply to your current study space?
2 What other tips can you think of for creating an effective study space?
3 What challenges do you think some people face when trying to set up a study space?

READING	Identifying the author's purpose Skimming
VOCABULARY	Organizing new words: nouns and verbs
WRITING	Understanding sentence patterns
GRAMMAR	Verbs followed by infinitives and gerunds

Discussion point

Discuss these questions with a partner.

1 Look at the picture. What can you see? What is it?

   In the picture I can see … . I think it's a …

2 Do you wear a watch? How often do you check the time?

   I always / never wear a watch because … . I check the time …

3 Are you ever late for class? Why or why not?

   I'm always / sometimes / never late for class because …

Vocabulary preview

Read these sentences. (Circle) the correct meanings of the words in bold.

1 That clock is not **accurate**. It says it is noon but it is really 12:10.
   a correct in every detail   **b** easy to see

2 When you are busy, it is good to **prioritize** and do the important things first.
   a put in order of importance   **b** do several things at the same time

3 Cristina is a very **punctual** person. She is always on time.
   a arriving unexpectedly   **b** arriving at the right time

4 I am always early for class. My teacher can **rely on** me.
   a trust   **b** play on

5 It is time for my medical check-up. I need to **schedule** a doctor's appointment.
   a plan   **b** cancel

6 Do not **skip** class. You will miss important information for the exam.
   a be absent from   **b** stay late at

7 Telling the time is very **straightforward**. I learned when I was five.
   a difficult to understand   **b** not difficult to understand

READING 1 A matter of time

Before you read

1 **Do you ever read blogs? Why or why not? If so, which of the types in the box on the right do you read? What can people learn from blogs? Discuss with a partner.**

   I often / sometimes / never read blogs because ... .
   I think people can learn ... from blogs.

TYPES OF BLOG	
cooking	personal
corporate	sports
news	travel

2 **Preview *A matter of time*. Discuss these questions.**
   1 What is it about?
   2 What do you think the picture of the airplane clock represents?

Global reading

Read *A matter of time*. <u>Underline</u> the seven tips the blogger mentions.

Close reading

1 **Read these sentences. Write the tip number each person should consider in *A matter of time*.**

   a Khalid constantly checks his email while he studies.   ___
   b Jackie studies for long periods of time without getting up and moving around.   ___
   c Paul does several things at once. He loses his focus easily.   ___
   d Akemi always finds the time to help, even if her own work suffers.   ___
   e Jun completely forgot about an appointment and did not turn up.   ___
   f Clare is not always clear on what her goals are. She cannot see how much progress she has made.   ___
   g Hassan worked hard all day and did not have enough time to finish his most important project.   ___

IDENTIFYING THE AUTHOR'S PURPOSE

Every author has a purpose or reason in writing a text. Identifying the purpose will help you to understand the text. Purposes include: to entertain, to persuade, and to inform. Authors may have more than one purpose.

2 Check (✓) the author's main purpose in writing *A matter of time*.

1 ☐ inform   **2** ☐ entertain   **3** ☐ persuade

A MATTER OF TIME

Hi everyone! Last week was really stressful for me. I'm usually pretty punctual but was late to several of my classes. I forgot to do my homework and I failed to write my weekly blog post—sorry! I realized I have a problem with time, so I decided to do something about it. I did some research and got some advice from friends and teachers. I want to share simple, straightforward tips for better time management. I've already started doing these and I can see the difference!

1. WRITE IT DOWN
Don't rely on your memory to keep track of every little detail. Memory is not always accurate. Write down the things you need to do in a small notebook, or use an online tool to create and update your "to-do" list.

2. PRIORITIZE
Schedule important things first. Then plan other things around them. Think of it this way: You want to fit three large rocks, some smaller rocks, and some sand into a jar. If you put in the sand first, and then the smaller rocks, you won't have room for the big rocks. It's better to put the big rocks in first, then the smaller rocks, and finally the sand.

3. DON'T SKIP THE BREAKS
Working for long periods without a break can waste your time. It is more efficient to work or study for a shorter period of time, take a break, and then go back to work. You may get more done in two focused 45-minute sessions.

4. ONE THING AT A TIME
Every time we switch from one task to another, we lose focus. Do one thing at a time, and do it well. As the Chinese proverb says, "One cannot manage too many affairs. Like pumpkins in the water, one pops up while you try to hold down the other."

5. SCHEDULE EMAIL TIME
On my cell phone I get a notification every time someone sends me an email. So I check my email many, many times a day. Turn that notification off! Schedule time to check your email. It doesn't matter when.

6. CHOOSE TO SAY "NO"
It's easy to become overwhelmed if we say "yes" to everything. Think about the task before you commit to it. Do you need to do it? Can someone else do it? Avoid saying "yes" to every request. This takes time away from more important tasks.

7. KEEP A GOAL JOURNAL
Write down your goals in a journal and evaluate them regularly. Mark your progress for each goal. Be sure you take the necessary steps to achieve your goals.

What do you think? Are these helpful tips? Please post your thoughts!

ACADEMIC KEYWORDS		
create	(v)	/kriˈeɪt/
evaluate	(v)	/ɪˈvæljuˌeɪt/
simple	(adj)	/ˈsɪmp(ə)l/

Developing critical thinking

Discuss these questions in a group.

1 Which tips are the most helpful? Which are the least helpful?

I find / don't find the tip about ... helpful because ...

2 What other tips would be helpful for better time management?

Other helpful tips for better time management are ...

3 What kind of person do you think reads this blog? Use the useful words in the box on the right.

Someone who is ... probably reads this blog.

USEFUL WORDS	
busy	organized
hardworking	punctual
lazy	reliable

READING 2 What time is it?

Before you read

Try these two experiments.

1 What time is it right now? Write down the exact time. Then compare with the people around you. How do you explain any differences?

I think we have the same / different times because ...

2 Look at the second hand of a clock, or use a stopwatch. Close your eyes and count 60 seconds. When you think exactly one minute has passed, check the clock. How accurate were you? Why do you think that is?

I was / wasn't very accurate because ...

Global reading

> **SKIMMING**
>
> Skimming is when you read a text quickly to get a general idea of what it is about. It also helps you figure out how difficult the text is going to be and how much time it will take to read.
>
> You do not read every word. Like previewing (unit 1), look at the title, headings, photos, captions, charts, and the first line of each paragraph. Let your eyes move quickly over the text.

Skim *What time is it?* Check (✓) what it is about.

1 ☐ Early Egyptian clocks
2 ☐ A history of clocks
3 ☐ Why clocks are not accurate

Close reading

1 **Match the clocks with when they were invented.**

1	mechanical clock	___	a	1956
2	sundial	___	b	1927
3	digital clock	___	c	the 13th century
4	water clock	___	d	3,400 years ago
5	quartz clock	___	e	3,500 years ago
6	sun clock	___	f	5,500 years ago

2 **Write the answers to these questions.**

1 Why was the sundial an improvement over the sun clock?
2 What was one problem with both the sun clock and sundial?
3 Where were water clocks used?
4 When did clocks begin to be more accurate?
5 What improved the accuracy of the mechanical clock?
6 When did people start to rely on clocks to run businesses?

WHAT TIME IS IT?

[1] How do we know the time? Look around. Is there a clock on the wall? Are you wearing a watch? Does your cell phone show the time? Telling the time is straightforward these days and essential if we want to schedule things and be punctual, but it was not always so easy. Many years ago there were no clocks. Over the centuries, people have developed different ways of telling the time.

[2] About 5,500 years ago, the Egyptians invented the sun clock. This was a tall stone structure. Its shadow marked the movement of the sun. They were able to determine midday and measure time from these shadows.

[3] About 3,500 years ago, the Egyptians made a sundial. The sundial was smaller than the sun clock and could measure time for half a day. After midday, they had to move it 180 degrees to measure the afternoon hours. On cloudy days or at night it was impossible to tell time with a sun clock or a sundial.

[4] Water clocks were the first clocks not to use the sun. The idea is simple. Water flows from one container to another at a constant rate. When the water reaches a certain level, it moves a lever and this shows the hours. The Egyptians used water clocks about 3,400 years ago. These clocks were popular in the Middle East and China but they failed to keep accurate time.

[5] In the 13th century, the mechanical clock was invented. This was more accurate, but was expensive to make. Over the next few centuries the design was developed. For example, springs were added around 1500. This improved accuracy and allowed clocks to be smaller. Mechanical clocks continued to develop until they had an accuracy of one-hundredth of a second per day.

[6] In 1927, the first quartz clock was developed. A quartz clock is accurate because of the regular vibration that occurs when an electric current is run through the mineral quartz. Clocks became cheaper to build and own. People began relying on them more and more to run businesses, transportation, and markets.

[7] More recently, in 1956, came the digital clock. And nowadays satellites send our cell phones the time to the exact second. There have been a lot of advances in timekeeping but some things never change. Many of us still have trouble getting out of bed on time and not missing appointments.

Developing critical thinking

1 Discuss these questions in a group.

1 What other ways of measuring time can you name? What other things help with time management?

You can also measure time using ...
There are many things to help you manage your time, such as ...

2 Do you think clocks make life easier or more difficult?

I think clocks make life easier / more difficult because ...

2 Think about the ideas from *A matter of time* and *What time is it?* and discuss these questions in a group.

1 Why is time management important at school and in the workplace?

Time management is important at school because ...

2 What other skills and strengths are important in school? Think about the things in the box on the right.

Although time management is very important, I think ... is also important because ...

ACADEMIC KEYWORDS

different	(adj)	/ˈdɪf(ə)rənt/
fail	(v)	/feɪl/
level	(n)	/ˈlev(ə)l/

THINK ABOUT:

computer literacy   motivation
confidence   organization
hard work   punctuality

Vocabulary skill

ORGANIZING NEW WORDS: NOUNS AND VERBS

One way to organize new words is to think about parts of speech. Two of the most common parts of speech are nouns and verbs.

<u>Nouns</u> describe a person, place, or thing.

*Is there a **clock** on the **wall**?*

*The **Egyptians** invented the **sundial**.*

<u>Verbs</u> describe an action or state.

*How **do** we **know** the time?*

*Clocks **became** cheaper to **build** and **own**.*

1 Read these sentences from *A matter of time*. Write *N* (noun) or *V* (verb) for the words in bold.

1 I did some **research**. _____

2 **Schedule** important things first. _____

3 Working for long periods without a break can **waste** your time. _____

4 Every time we switch from one task to another, we lose **focus**. _____

5 I check my **email** many, many times a day. _____

6 Avoid saying yes to every **request**. _____

7 Mark your **progress** for each goal. _____

8 Please **post** your thoughts! _____

2 Read these sentences from *What time is it?* Circle the nouns. <u>Underline</u> the verbs.

1 Are you wearing a watch?

2 Many years ago there were no clocks.

3 Its shadow marked the movement of the sun.

4 They were able to determine midday.

5 After midday, they had to move it 180 degrees.

6 At night it was impossible to tell time.

7 These clocks were popular in the Middle East.

8 Over the next few centuries the design was developed.

3 Read this post to the blog *A matter of time*. Complete the word web with nine nouns and nine verbs.

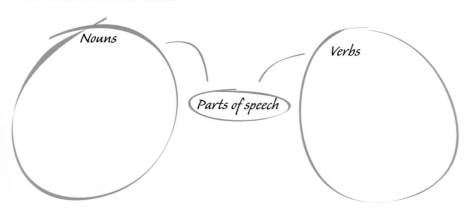

22 AUG   POST 14

I rarely read blogs, but I really enjoyed your recent post. The information was very useful. I have a lot of stress in my life and I know that I manage my time poorly. The advice about breaks was a great idea! I want to thank you!

WRITING Describing how to achieve a goal

You are going to learn about writing basic sentence patterns and verbs that can be followed by infinitives and gerunds. You are then going to use these to write a paragraph describing how to achieve a goal you set for yourself.

Writing skill

UNDERSTANDING SENTENCE PATTERNS

In its simplest form, a sentence in English consists of a subject (a noun or pronoun) and a verb. Patterns can also include adjectives, adverbs, or prepositional phrases. Study these common patterns:

Subject + verb (S + V)

I write.

Subject + verb + direct object (S + V + DO)

He has a time management problem.

He has a lot of time.

Subject + verb + indirect object + direct object (S + V + IO + DO)

She gave him some advice.

He sent me an email.

Sentences are the building blocks of writing. By understanding and using a variety of sentence patterns, you will make your writing more varied and interesting to read.

1 **Write the sentence pattern for these sentences. Use the sentence patterns in the box.**

   S + V   S + V + DO   S + V + IO + DO

   1 Many people struggle with time management.   _____
   2 Jessica took a long study break.   _____
   3 Michael has never kept a goal journal.   _____
   4 I just sent you an interesting web link.   _____
   5 Nadia does not blog regularly.   _____
   6 That article has given me some interesting ideas. _____

2 **Unscramble these sentences. Then write the sentence pattern.**

   1 to / skip / Kevin / plans / class
   2 refuses / text / Sachiko / to
   3 his / Lucas / relies on / cell phone
   4 has / me / emails / Omar /sent / five

Grammar

VERBS FOLLOWED BY INFINITIVES AND GERUNDS

Certain verbs can be followed by an infinitive and others can be followed by a gerund. Some verbs can be followed by either an infinitive or a gerund with little or no change in meaning. Study the forms:

Form	Example
Verbs followed by infinitives verb* + *to* + base form *verbs that can be followed by an infinitive include: *agree, ask, appear, be able, choose, decide, expect, fail, hope, plan, seem, want*	They decided to make a water clock. I failed to write my weekly blog.
Verbs followed by gerunds verb* + verb *-ing* *verbs that can be followed by a gerund include: *admit, appreciate, avoid, consider, deny, dislike, enjoy, finish, imagine, keep, practice, quit*	I dislike being late. Avoid saying yes to every request.
Verbs followed by infinitives or gerunds verb* + *to* + base form / verb *-ing* * verbs that can be followed by an infinitive or a gerund include: *begin, cannot stand, continue, hate, like, love, prefer, start*	Clocks continued to develop. Clocks continued developing.

1 Complete these sentences. Use the infinitive or gerund form of the verb in parentheses. Write both if either is possible.

1 If you are not able _____ (understand) something right away, do not give up. Keep _____ (work) until you understand it.

2 We all may need _____ (miss) a class sometimes but avoid _____ (skip) class.

3 If you need help in class, ask _____ (speak) to your teacher.

4 Practice _____ (write) down new words as you learn them.

5 Many students like _____ (keep) a vocabulary notebook.

6 Quit _____ (study) 30–60 minutes before you go to bed.

2 Complete this conversation. Use the infinitive or gerund form of the verbs in the box.

continue	do	get	reduce	take	think

Amany: How many classes did you decide (1) _____ next semester?

Lisa: I chose (2) _____ my classes from six to five. What do you want (3) _____ after graduation?

Amany: I'd like (4) _____ my studies. What about you?

Lisa: I have no idea.

Amany: Have you considered (5) _____ a job right away?

Lisa: Of course. But I don't like (6) _____ about it. It gives me stress.

WRITING TASK

Read this paragraph. <u>Underline</u> the verbs + infinitive. (Circle) the verbs + gerund.

I like going for bike rides, and I love going for long walks. Unfortunately, I don't seem to have time for these things anymore. I'd like to have more free time for myself so I can do the things I enjoy doing. To achieve this, I will do several things. I plan to write down my appointments and then I will prioritize them. I hate to forget things, and this sometimes happens. I'll be more organized this way. I have a part-time job and I hope to reduce my hours from 15 to 12 hours per week. I also need to say "no" to my friends more. They often rely on me for homework help and I have to avoid saying "yes" every time. I want to be more honest and straightforward with them about my time commitments. If I achieve these things, I'll be able to have more free time.

BRAINSTORM

Read the goals in the box. Which one would you like to achieve? Why? What specific things can you do to achieve your goal? Complete the chart with your ideas.

| to balance work and play more | to be better at time management |
| to have less stress in my life | to have more free time for myself |

My goal

Why I'd like to achieve my goal

Specific things I can do to reach my goal
1
2
3
4

PLAN

Plan a paragraph describing how to achieve your goal. Look back at your brainstorm and write a topic sentence. Include at least three things you will do to achieve your goal.

WRITE

Write your paragraph. Include a variety of sentence patterns in your paragraph. Pay attention to your use of verbs followed by infinitives and gerunds.

SHARE

Exchange paragraphs with a partner. Look at the checklist on page 109 and provide feedback to your partner.

REWRITE AND EDIT

Consider your partner's comments and rewrite your paragraph.

Writing for the fearful

by Stella Cottrell

If you need to improve your writing skills, try some of the following short exercises.

Get the writing habit

- Write out a story you enjoyed as a child.
- Write to a friend saying what you hope to get out of being a student.
- Write down ten English words you like the sound of. Write a short piece which includes all those words. Be as crazy as you like.
- Play "Just a minute": give yourself one minute to write about one of the following:

  (a) The worst thing I ate …

  (b) The most embarrassing thing that ever happened …

  (c) I'm lucky because …

  (d) What annoys me is …

  (e) Anything you like.

Write for five minutes

1 Choose any subject.

2 Do not stop to think. The idea is to get used to writing continuously, whatever the content. Just write as much as you can.

3 When you can write for five minutes, extend the time to ten minutes and build up your limit.

Write from prompts

pictures   photographs

dreams   things you see in the street

conversations with friends

Write about what you see, hear, think, or dream.

Make a life chart

- Include important events in your childhood, family, education, interests, work, and so on.
- Write a few lines about each item.
- Choose one item and write about this in more detail. Describe what happened, how you felt about it at the time, how it affected you in the long term, whether what happened was unusual, and so on.

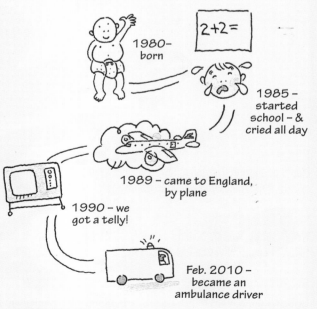

1980– born

1985 – started school – & cried all day

1989 – came to England, by plane

1990 – we got a telly!

Feb. 2010 – became an ambulance driver

LIFE CHART

Discussion point

Discuss these questions with a partner.

1 Look at the picture. What do you think the homes are like inside?

The homes might be ...

2 What is the best thing about your home? Why?

The best thing about my home is ... because ...

3 What kind of home would you like to have someday?

Someday, I would like to have ...

READING	Highlighting Annotating
VOCABULARY	Using explanations to find meaning
WRITING	Brainstorming word maps
GRAMMAR	*There is / are* (+ quantifier) + noun

Vocabulary preview

Read this paragraph about people in Mongolia. Circle the correct words in bold.

About a third of Mongolia's people are nomads, moving from place to place with no fixed (1) **direction / location** to call home. They are famous for their (2) **distinctive / common** way of dressing, their horses, and the yurts they continue to live in. A (3) **rare / typical** nomad family has about seven members and follows a seasonal (4) **timetable / routine**. They move four times a year, depending on the availability of (5) **light / resources**. Their (6) **lifestyle / happiness** involves raising livestock such as sheep, cattle, and camels. There are many (7) **traditions / movements** related to nomadic culture. One (8) **common / unique** festival only found in Mongolia is *Naadam*, consisting of sports such as wrestling, horse racing, and archery.

READING 1   Home is where the heart is

Before you read

Read these common sayings in English. What do they mean to you? Do you have similar sayings in your own language? Discuss with a partner.

> **"There is no place like home."**

> **"Home follows the family."**   **"Love makes a house a home."**

> **"Home is where the heart is."**

To me, this saying means ...
We have a similar saying in ... . It means ...

Global reading

Skim *Home is where the heart is*. Circle what each paragraph is about.

Paragraph 1	**a** What nomads are	**b** Who Ibrahim is
Paragraph 2	**a** The Bedouin	**b** How many nomads there are and where they live
Paragraph 3	**a** The Tuareg lifestyle	**b** The Tuareg diet
Paragraph 4	**a** Tuareg homes	**b** Tuareg marriage
Paragraph 5	**a** Tuareg children	**b** Pressure on Tuareg lifestyles

Close reading

> **HIGHLIGHTING**
>
> When you skim a text (unit 2), you can highlight important information. This means you read the text more closely and it will help you to remember the information. It also makes the text easier to read and review later.
>
> Highlight the most important parts. Every text is different, but you should highlight no more than 10%.

1 Read *Home is where the heart is*. Highlight the most important information. Then compare in a group. Discuss these questions.

  1 Did you highlight similar information?
  2 What differences did you find?

2 Write *T* (true), *F* (false), or *NG* (not given).

1 In the past, there were more nomadic cultures. ____

2 The Tuareg are the largest nomadic group in the world. ____

3 Today, most Tuareg do not lead a nomadic lifestyle. ____

4 The "Blue Men" got their name from their blue clothing. ____

5 It does not take long to take down or put up a Tuareg tent. ____

6 Men are responsible for the family tent. ____

7 Tourism is beginning to affect the Tuareg lifestyle. ____

8 More Tuareg are moving to cities to look for jobs. ____

3 Compare your answers with a partner. Discuss these questions.

1 Find the answers to exercise 2 in the text. Is the information highlighted?

2 Was highlighting helpful?

ACADEMIC KEYWORDS		
culture	(n)	/ˈkʌltʃər/
define	(v)	/dɪˈfaɪn/
pressure	(n)	/ˈpreʃər/

HOME IS WHERE THE HEART IS

1 As dawn breaks at the edge of the Sahara, Ibrahim and his wife Miriam are packing up their home. They and other Tuareg families are moving to a new location. This routine is typical. Their life, like the life of all nomads, is one of movement.

2 There are nomadic people in Africa and Central Asia, with a number of reindeer herders above the Arctic Circle and some Bedouin in the Middle East. Many cultures were once nomadic but these days the numbers are smaller, though there are still 30 to 40 million nomads in the world. It is not known how many Tuareg there are, but estimates range from 1 million to 1.5 million.

3 The Tuareg live in the Saharan regions of North and West Africa, in Niger, Mali, Burkina Faso, Algeria, and Libya. Most lead a nomadic lifestyle based on trade and livestock, raising goats, sheep, cattle, and camels. The men are sometimes called "Blue Men" because of their distinctive blue clothing. The blue cloth protects the men's face from the sun and sand. It also stains their skin and defines their unique identity.

4 Tuareg families live in camps. The homes of the Tuareg are simple tents. They usually have a light wood frame and are covered with animal skins or mats. This makes it easy to take the tent down and put it up in a new location. When a woman marries, her family makes a tent for her. This belongs to her and she is responsible for its care.

5 At one time the Tuareg were responsible for transporting goods across the Sahara. Nowadays, customs and traditions are changing. The loss of resources and a growing population is putting pressure on their nomadic lifestyle. More and more Tuareg people are starting to farm, and some are moving to cities to work. But many Tuareg, like other nomads around the world, are keeping to their traditional way of life.

Developing critical thinking

Discuss these questions in a group.

1 What do you think are the advantages and disadvantages of a nomadic lifestyle? Think about the things in the box on the right.

Advantages	Disadvantages
close family ties	

2 Would you like to live a nomadic lifestyle? Why or why not?

I would / wouldn't like to live a nomadic lifestyle. I think it would be ...

3 Describe the type of lifestyle you think you will have in the future. Consider the areas in question 1.

For me, the lifestyle that appeals most is one with ... because ...

READING 2 Home automation

Before you read

Which of the gadgets or appliances in the box on the right do you have around your house? What do you use them for? Discuss with a partner.

We have ... in our house. We use it for ...

Global reading

Skim *Home automation*. Check (✓) the best sub-title.

1 ☐ Everyday home features
2 ☐ The smartest home in the world
3 ☐ Microsoft's Ian Mercer
4 ☐ How to make your home smarter

Close reading

1 **Read *Home automation*. Highlight at least ten things that Ian Mercer's home does.**

Tablet

> ### ◼ ANNOTATING ◼
>
> If you highlight a text, you mark the most important information. As you read more closely, it is also useful to annotate text. This helps you stay focused on, understand, and remember the text.
>
> There is no fixed way to annotate text, but try these techniques:
> - <u>Underline</u> new vocabulary and write definitions in the margins.
> - Write questions in the margins next to where the answer is found.
> - Ⓒircle major claims or important statistics.
> - Put an exclamation mark (!) next to things you have a strong reaction to.
> - Put a question mark (?) next to things that are unclear, for checking.

Microwave

Telephone

2 Read this annotated paragraph. Then read and annotate *Home automation*.

Who is Ian Mercer? Ian Mercer doesn't set an alarm clock. The former Microsoft senior manager doesn't check the weather, either. He doesn't turn on lights, water *change* the yard, or adjust the thermostat. He doesn't = *temperature controls* open the curtains, answer the phone, or call his children for dinner. There's something unique about Ian's home! He has programmed it to do all these things for him?

3 Compare your annotations in a group. Discuss these questions.
1 Did you make similar annotations?
2 What differences did you find?

ACADEMIC KEYWORDS

activity	(n)	/æk'tɪvəti/
control	(v)	/kən'troʊl/
normal	(adj)	/nɔrm(ə)l/

Home automation

[1] Ian Mercer doesn't set an alarm clock. The former Microsoft senior manager doesn't check the weather, either. He doesn't turn on lights, water the yard, or adjust the thermostat. He doesn't open the curtains, answer the phone, or call his children for dinner. There's something unique about Ian's home. He has programmed it to do all these things for him.

[2] Ian doesn't live in a typical home or have a typical lifestyle. He spent over a decade designing the systems that feature in his distinctive home. He started by buying a home automation software package. He then started to modify it.

[3] After all these changes there are now 79 sensors and monitors and 48 light switches in his home. Lights turn on automatically in rooms with people in them. No one has to turn them on. Ian can also control his home remotely using voice commands or his phone. He doesn't need to be at home to do so. He can be in any location. That is only the beginning of what this home has been programmed to do.

[4] It interfaces with online calendars, caller ID, online weather services, online address books, and email, among other things, to get Ian through his day. For example, if there is a meeting in Ian's calendar it will wake him up, open his bedroom curtains, start and set his shower to his desired temperature, and turn on the TV news. Ian has also programmed his home to recognize normal routines and plans. It can also recognize if there are more people than normal and reacts by turning up the air conditioning.

[5] There is plenty more this home has been programmed to do. It monitors local weather and informs Ian about traffic conditions. It keeps him updated on his favorite sports teams and scores. It even monitors online activity to check that Ian's children are doing their homework. The "dinner's ready" command suspends operation of their computers and TVs. This is easier than asking his children to shut them down.

[6] Ian's home is unique. Most homes are not this smart, but soon more homes will be technologically advanced. Your refrigerator may soon be programmed to monitor what you use and create a grocery list, or order the food automatically. Smart air conditioning systems will be able to keep you comfortable and save money.

Developing critical thinking

1 Discuss these questions in a group.

1 Which of the characteristics in the box on the right would you use to describe Ian Mercer? Why?

I think Ian Mercer is ... because ...

2 Would you like to live in a smart home? Why or why not?

I would / wouldn't like to live in a smart home. I think it would be ...

CHARACTERISTICS	
amazing	rich
interesting	smart
lazy	strange

2 Think about the ideas from *Home is where the heart is* and *Home automation* and discuss these questions in a group.

1 What do you think all people look for in a home? Think about the things in the box on the right.

I think most people look for ... because ... . I would look for ...

2 How much do you think someone's home affects their lifestyle?

Someone's home affects his or her lifestyle a lot / a little because ...

THINK ABOUT:	
age	price
comfort	size
location	style

Vocabulary skill

USING EXPLANATIONS TO FIND MEANING

In addition to using examples to help you find the meaning of new words (unit 1), you can look for explanations. An explanation can come either before or after a word.

It's a good idea to consult with a professional before you purchase home automation software. Asking for specialist advice will save you time and money.

("Asking for specialist advice" gives the meaning of "consult")

1 Read these sentences from *Home automation*. Write the definitions of the words in bold.

1 He then started to **modify** it. After all these changes there are now 79 sensors and monitors and 48 light switches in the home.

modify = _____

2 Ian can also control his home **remotely** using voice commands or his phone. He doesn't need to be at home to do so.

remotely = _____

3 The "dinner's ready" command **suspends** operation of their computers and TVs. This is easier than asking his children to shut them down.

suspends = _____

2 Read these sentences about home automation. Write the definitions of the words in bold.

1 Remote controls operate up to 40 meters away. This **range** is high, but recent advances are increasing the area covered even more.

range = _____

2 Some home automation products may not be **compatible** with others. Always check to make sure a new product will work with your existing ones.

compatible = _____

3 It takes time for things to develop, and home automation will continue to **evolve**.

evolve = _____

WRITING Describing your home

You are going to learn about brainstorming word maps for ideas for
writing, and using *there is / are*. You are then going to use these to write a
paragraph describing your home.

Writing skill

BRAINSTORMING WORD MAPS

When you brainstorm ideas for writing, it is useful to use a word map to
write down what comes to mind.

Begin with a key word in a circle. From that word generate a web of ideas,
adding related words as your word map grows. Study this partial word map
for the topic "Tuareg tents":

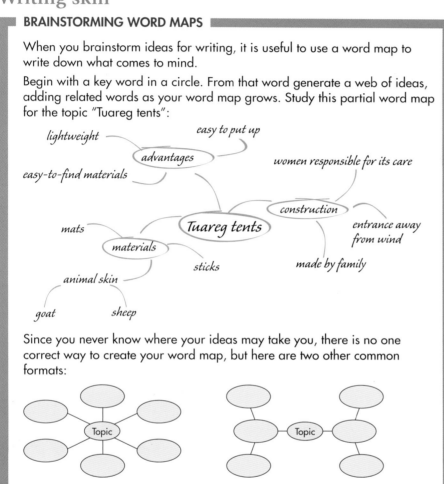

Since you never know where your ideas may take you, there is no one
correct way to create your word map, but here are two other common
formats:

1 Create a word map for a paragraph describing your family.

2 Compare your word map with a partner. What differences do you see?

Grammar

THERE IS / ARE (+ QUANTIFIER) + NOUN

There + is/are indicates that something exists, or is in a certain location. You can add a quantifier between *is/are* and the noun to give more information. Study the forms:

Form	Example
Singular count nouns	
There is + singular count noun	There is a meeting today.
There is + quantifier* + singular count noun	There is one meeting today.
Plural count nouns	
There are + plural count noun	There are nomadic people all over the world.
There are + quantifier* + plural count noun	There are many nomadic people all over the world.
Noncount nouns	
There is + noncount noun	There is privacy in my house.
There is + quantifier** + noncount noun	There is a great deal of privacy in my house.

Quantifiers that can go before a …
*count noun: *a, a couple, a few, a large number of , a lot of, lots, (not) many, no, not any, one, plenty of, several, some, three*
**noncount noun: *a great deal of, a little, a lot of, lots, not any, no, not much, plenty of, some*

1 Complete these sentences. Use *is* or *are*.

1 There _____ a yard behind my house.
2 There _____ a large number of windows in my living room.
3 There _____ three bedrooms in my house.
4 There _____ a lot of street noise in front of my house.
5 There _____ plenty of light in the kitchen.
6 There _____ a couple of new homes down the street.
7 There _____ a lot of traffic in my neighborhood.
8 There _____ some fun things to do in my neighborhood.

2 Circle the correct quantifier in bold.

1 There is **one** / **several** bathroom in my house.
2 There is not **many** / **much** space in my closet.
3 There are only a **few** / **little** empty apartments in my building.
4 There is a **large number of** / **great deal of** crime around here.
5 Why is there **a** / **some** car in front of my house?
6 There are **some** / **any** home improvements I want to make.
7 Is there **a** / **many** laundry room in your house?
8 Are they **many** / **much** bedrooms in your house?

3 Read the sentences in exercise 1. Which are true for you?

WRITING TASK

Read this paragraph. <u>Underline</u> the nouns after *there is* and *there are*.
(Circle) any quantifiers.

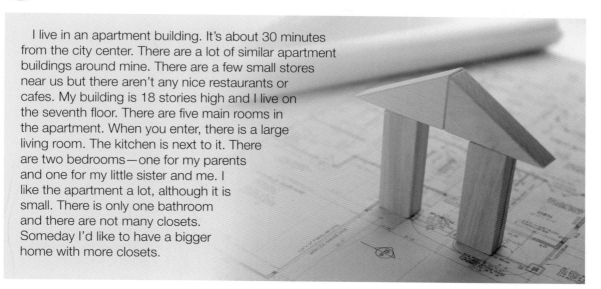

I live in an apartment building. It's about 30 minutes from the city center. There are a lot of similar apartment buildings around mine. There are a few small stores near us but there aren't any nice restaurants or cafes. My building is 18 stories high and I live on the seventh floor. There are five main rooms in the apartment. When you enter, there is a large living room. The kitchen is next to it. There are two bedrooms—one for my parents and one for my little sister and me. I like the apartment a lot, although it is small. There is only one bathroom and there are not many closets. Someday I'd like to have a bigger home with more closets.

BRAINSTORM

Think about your home. Where is it? What does it look like? What is it near? What rooms does it have? Complete the word map with your ideas.

My home

PLAN

Plan a paragraph describing your home. Look back at your brainstorm and write a topic sentence. Decide how to organize your paragraph.

WRITE

Write your paragraph. Pay attention to your use of *there is / are* (+ quantifier) + noun.

SHARE

Exchange paragraphs with a partner. Look at the checklist on page 109 and provide feedback to your partner.

REWRITE AND EDIT

Consider your partner's comments and rewrite your paragraph.

STUDY SKILLS Reviewing and practicing vocabulary

Getting started

Try this experiment. Study the Group 1 words for one minute. Then close your book and write the words you remember. Do the same for Group 2. Did you remember more words from Group 1 or 2? Why?

Group 1

orange	window	student	sad
wide	help	name	house
sky	shirt	play	book
clock	water	tall	lunch

Group 2

desk	chalk	teacher	class
blue	green	pink	yellow
glad	happy	pleased	joyful
thick	thin	wide	narrow

Scenario

Read this scenario. Think about what Lucy is doing right and what she is doing wrong.

Consider it

Read these five tips for how to remember new words. Discuss each one with a partner. Which can you do alone? Which are better to do with others?

1 **Read** Reading a lot is one of the best ways to learn new words. Most words are learned from context. As you read, pay attention to words you do not know and try to use the context to guess their meaning.

2 **Be active** You will not learn many new words by simply studying lists. Be more active. Write the definition and example sentence. Draw a picture of the word. Say it aloud. Use it in a sentence. And keep everything in a vocabulary notebook.

3 **Categorize** The human brain likes to classify things. Take advantage of this by categorizing related words. Word families are easier to learn than unrelated words. For example, under *Furniture* you might group *sofa, closet, armchair, bed*, etc.

4 **Same and different** We can remember similar and opposite meanings more easily because they "stick together" in our minds. For example, learn *honest, trustworthy* (a synonym), and *dishonest* (an antonym) at the same time.

5 **Review** Research shows that people need to see a word at least ten times before they truly understand and remember it. Review often with others by quizzing one another or playing word games.

Over to you

Discuss these questions with a partner.

1 Think back to the experiment above. Which tips were used for Group 2?

2 Which of the tips do you use to remember new words?

3 What other things do you do to learn vocabulary? How effective are they?

Lucy is trying to improve her vocabulary. When she reads, she underlines every new word. The next day she looks up the underlined words in a dictionary. She then writes the words in an alphabetical list in a notebook. Next to each word she writes the definition and an example sentence. Sometimes she even draws a picture of the new word. She reviews her vocabulary list often but feels frustrated because she has trouble remembering many of the words she has written down.

Size

READING	Predicting Making inferences
VOCABULARY	Using definitions to find meaning
WRITING	Writing compound sentences
GRAMMAR	The present progressive tense

Discussion point

Discuss these questions with a partner.

1   Look at the picture. What can you see? Can you name other big and
    small animals that live together?

    The picture shows ...

2   Is your town or city big or small? How big is your country?

    My town is ... . My country is ...

3   Which of these sayings do you agree with more? Why?

    "Good things come in small packages."   "Bigger is better."

    I agree with the saying ... more, because I feel ...

Vocabulary preview

1 In each set, match the words with their meanings.

1 abundant ___   a except for

2 approximately ___   b a large number of things in one area

3 aside from ___   c the amount of something that people want

4 concentration ___   d not exactly

5 demand ___   e available in large quantities

6 efficient ___   f first / most important

7 massive ___   g working well and producing good results

8 population ___   h very large

9 primary ___   i all the people or animals that live in an area

2 Complete these sentences. Use the words in exercise 1.

1 Tuna used to be _____ but their numbers have decreased recently.

2 There is low _____ for new homes because of the poor economy.

3 The penguin _____ has declined sharply over the past 30 years.

4 The Pacific Ocean is _____. It covers a third of the Earth's surface.

5 _____ last year's typhoon, we have not had any serious storms.

6 Fish is not the penguin's _____ source of food.

7 At birth, a baby elephant weighs _____ 100 kilograms.

8 This lightweight boat is very _____. It does not use much energy.

9 Isla Mujeres in Mexico is home to a large _____ of whale sharks.

READING 1 Fuel of the sea

Before you read

1 What do blue whales eat? How many kilograms of food do blue whales eat a day? Why are some penguin populations decreasing in number? Discuss your predictions with a partner.

I think blue whales eat ...
They might eat ... kilograms of food a day.
Perhaps some penguin populations are decreasing in number because ...

> **PREDICTING**
>
> Before you read, you can use the title, pictures, headings, and your own personal experience to make predictions about the text. Predicting also involves thinking while you read, checking, and further refining and revising your predictions.
>
> It is an important skill because activating prior background knowledge allows you to connect the new information with what you already know. This makes the new information easier to understand and remember.

2 Preview *Fuel of the sea*. Check (✓) your prediction for what the title means.

1 ☐ Krill are a fuel that may solve our energy problems.

2 ☐ Krill are a primary food source for many sea animals.

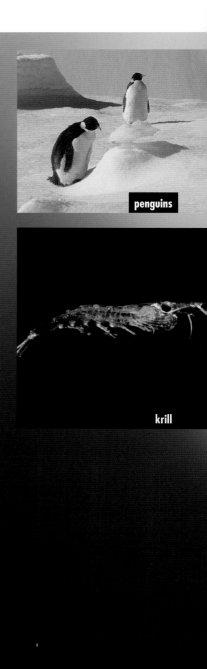

penguins

krill

Global reading

Skim *Fuel of the sea.* **Check your prediction.**

Close reading

1 **Read** *Fuel of the sea.* **Check your guesses to** *Before you read* **exercise 1. Correct any wrong answers.**

2 **Highlight the important information and annotate** *Fuel of the sea.* **Then write the answers to these questions.**

   1 What are krill?
   2 Where do krill live?
   3 What animals eat them?
   4 How large can krill swarms get?
   5 What things are causing krill numbers to decline?
   6 What has happened as a result of this decline?

ACADEMIC KEYWORDS		
contain	(v)	/kən'teɪn/
force	(v)	/fɔrs/
recent	(adj)	/'risənt/

[1] Two blue whales are swimming up from the ocean depths. They are blowing bubbles in a tighter and tighter circle. Suddenly, one opens its huge mouth and takes in a massive amount of water. With a tongue that weighs more than an adult elephant, it forces the water out of its mouth. Using a highly efficient filtering system, it keeps and swallows hundreds of kilograms of krill. Krill are the primary source of food for many whales, and blue whales, the largest animal on earth, eat about four tons of krill every day.

[2] Krill are tiny, shrimp-like animals about the size of a paper clip. They spend their day in the ocean depths and rise to the surface each night to feed. They feed on phytoplankton—single-cell plants at the bottom of the food chain—and on algae found under sea ice. There are approximately 90 known species of krill. They are found in all the world's oceans and may live up to ten years. Aside from whales, many other sea animals such as fish, seals, and penguins depend on krill as a primary food source. This is why they are sometimes described as the fuel of the sea. Without krill, many of the life forms in the oceans would disappear.

[3] Normally krill are found in concentrations of 10 to 100 individuals per cubic meter. When they gather together in a defensive group called a swarm they may number up to 100,000 per cubic meter. A single swarm can be as large as 450 square kilometers and contain up to 200 million metric tons of krill. It can turn the surface of the ocean pink. Some swarms are large enough to be seen from space. Krill are so abundant that they weigh more than all of the people on Earth.

[4] Despite their huge numbers and long lives, recent studies by marine biologists have found that krill populations are declining. In the ocean around Antarctica their numbers have dropped as much as 80%. This is partly due to the loss of sea ice. Krill oil has become popular in dietary supplements in recent years, and this demand is also impacting krill numbers. Only a few countries currently fish for krill, but the numbers are growing. Some animals that feed on krill, such as penguins, have declined in number as a result.

[5] An individual krill may seem insignificant, but as a species they represent one of the most abundant and important animals on earth. Healthy krill populations in the future depend on the actions of students studying marine biology today, as well as the actions of everyday people.

Fuel *of the* sea

Developing critical thinking

Discuss these questions in a group.

1 What could marine biologists do to reverse the decline in krill numbers?

I think marine biologists could ...

2 What could everyday people do?

Everyday people could ...

3 How will you be affected if krill numbers continue to decline?

If krill numbers continue to decline, it will mean that ...

READING 2 Size doesn't matter

Before you read

1 **Look at the picture. What country is circled? What continent is it in? What is the most widely spoken language?**

I think the country is ... . It's in ... . The most widely spoken language is ...

2 **Think about the characteristics of a successful country in the box on the right. Which are most important? Why? Discuss with a partner.**

I think the most important characteristics are ... because ...

3 **Preview *Size doesn't matter*. Check (✓) what you think it is about.**

1 ☐ Why Singaporeans prefer to live in smaller homes.

2 ☐ How Singapore became successful even with little land.

3 ☐ What Singapore is doing to stop its population from growing.

Global reading

Skim *Size doesn't matter*. Check your predictions.

Close reading

1 **Read *Size doesn't matter*. Complete these sentences. Use the numbers in the box.**

3	15.5	100	7,300	24,000

1 About _____% of the people in Singapore are millionaires.

2 There are about _____ people per square kilometer in Singapore.

3 A typical neighborhood in Singapore consists of about _____ people.

4 Singapore has added about _____ square kilometers of reclaimed land.

5 Singapore has an unemployment rate of about _____%.

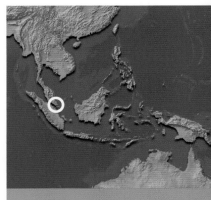

THINK ABOUT:

a common language
a good location
a large population
a lot of land
a pleasant climate
abundant resources
educated people
healthy people

MAKING INFERENCES

Writers do not always state everything directly. They may provide hints or clues that require you to *infer* meaning. When you make inferences, you go beyond the surface details of a text to interpret information and draw logical conclusions. We make inferences every day. For example, if someone enters a room shaking a wet umbrella, we can infer that it is raining outside.

2 Check (✓) the statements you can infer from *Size doesn't matter.*

1 ☐ Singapore does not have enough land to grow all of its food.
2 ☐ Singapore is a densely populated country.
3 ☐ Land reclamation is a good way to cope with a growing population.
4 ☐ Many people in Singapore use public transportation.
5 ☐ The population of Singapore is growing faster now than in the 1960s.
6 ☐ Unemployment will double if more people move to Singapore.

ACADEMIC KEYWORDS

additional	(adj)	/əˈdɪʃ(ə)nəl/
refer	(v)	/rɪˈfɜr/
system	(n)	/ˈsɪstəm/

Size doesn't matter

In 1960, the Housing Development Board (HDB) was founded. Within a decade, 50,000 new homes were built. Urban planning is now under the control of the Urban Redevelopment Authority (URA). Because there are about 7,300 people per square kilometer, about 85% of the population is now living in high-rise public housing units. These are referred to as housing estate towns and are divided into neighborhoods of about 24,000 people. Each neighborhood has schools, clinics, and many other businesses.

³ Singapore has a land reclamation project that builds up additional land from the sea floor. Engineers work to figure out where they can add to existing land in a way that will not affect tidal zones or water levels. The country has added about 100 square kilometers of land and is planning at least that much more in the near future. In fact, Singapore's famous Changi Airport is built on reclaimed land.

⁴ Transportation in Singapore is also well planned. Its Mass Rapid Transit system allows all areas to be accessed easily by rail, reducing road use substantially. Bus stations and train stations are built over each other to make efficient use of space and allow ease of access between transportation modes.

¹ Singapore is home to approximately five million people in an area of only about 700 square kilometers. It does not have abundant resources and was once a massive swamp. It imports much of its water and nearly all of its food. Yet Singapore enjoys excellent education and health systems, low taxes, and a per capita income greater than that of most countries. In fact, at 15.5%, the country has the highest concentration of millionaires on earth. How did such a small country, now one of the most urban countries in the world, manage to get so much right? Let us take a look, beginning with housing.

² Like any large city, Singapore has faced a growing population, and with it the high demand for housing.

⁵ Singapore has done a very good job of planning and designing its future, and it has paid off. Singapore has had an annual growth rate in its gross domestic product of about 8% since 1965, unemployment is always down around 3%, and personal savings are very strong. Aside from its primary industries of finance, manufacturing, and communications, Singapore is working toward being a global leader in information technology. Its citizens are among the best educated in the world. Singapore's future looks very bright indeed.

Developing critical thinking

1 Discuss these questions in a group.

1 How is Singapore similar to your town or city? How is it different? Think about the things in the box on the right.

My town and Singapore are very similar. They both have ...
My city has ... but Singapore has ...

2 Would you like to live in Singapore? Why or why not?

I would / wouldn't like to live in Singapore because ...

THINK ABOUT:

houses	size
industry	stores
population	train system

2 Think about the ideas from *Fuel of the sea* and *Size doesn't matter* and discuss these questions in a group.

1 Do you think it is better to live in a big city or a small town? Why?

I think it's better to live in ... because ...

2 Is it better for things to be big or small? Why? Think about the items in the box on the right.

For me, a ... university is better because ...

Vocabulary skill

USING DEFINITIONS TO FIND MEANING

In addition to using examples (unit 1) or explanations (unit 2) to help you find the meaning of new words, you can look for actual definitions.

Words that signal definitions: *means, consists of, defined as, described as, is / are, refers to, called, known as*

Definitions can also be set off by certain punctuation: within dashes — —, parentheses ( ), and commas , ,

THINK ABOUT:

a car	a home
a cell phone	a university
a computer	an airplane

1 Find these sentences in *Fuel of the sea*. Complete them with the correct definition or example.

1 Krill are _____ about the size of a paper clip.

2 They feed on phytoplankton—_____—and on algae found under sea ice.

3 Aside from whales, many other sea animals such as _____ depend on krill as a primary food source.

4 When they gather together in a defensive group called a _____ they may number up to 100,000 per cubic meter.

2 Complete these sentences about Singapore. Use the definitions in the box.

> a large, smelly, and spiky fruit
> a small country at the tip of the Malay Peninsula
> an island resort at the southern end of the country
> Indian, Chinese, and Malay influences
> one of the Asian "tigers"

1 Singapore, _____, is a popular tourist destination.

2 Sentosa Island—_____—is where Singaporeans go to relax.

3 The country's food consists of _____.

4 The durian (_____) is the national fruit of the country.

5 Singapore's economy is often referred to as _____.

3 Complete these definitions.

1 *Massive* is very _____.

2 *Approximately* means _____.

3 *Abundant* is defined as _____.

4 _____ refers to the amount of something that people want.

5 The people or animals that live in an area is known as its _____.

WRITING Describing how your neighborhood is changing

You are going to learn about writing compound sentences and using the present progressive tense. You are then going to use these to write a paragraph describing how your neighborhood is changing.

Writing skill

WRITING COMPOUND SENTENCES

A compound sentence contains two independent clauses, connected by a conjunction. Use *and* to link similar ideas, *but* to express a contrast, *or* to show a choice or possibility, and *so* to show a result.

English is Singapore's national language, **and** *many people speak it very well.*

Singapore consists of many islands, **but** *most of them are uninhabited.*

There is a bus that goes to Changi Airport, **or** *you can take a taxi.*

Singapore does not have much farmland, **so** *the government imports most food.*

We generally use commas in compound sentences but we may omit the comma if the sentence is very short, or the subjects are the same.

---

1 Read about Singapore neighborhoods. Circle the correct conjunctions in bold.

Singapore has many interesting neighborhoods. The Central Business District is located in the south, (1) **and / but** is where most of the country's skyscrapers are. There is a lot of traffic here during work hours, (2) **or / so** it's best to take public transportation if you plan to visit.

Also near downtown is The Riverside area. Go there for a nice meal, (3) **but / or** just walk along the river. The famous Orchard Road is known mostly for its shopping malls. There are many hotels there too, (4) **but / so** it's easy for tourists to simply walk out their hotels and shop.

Another neighborhood is Bugis and Kampong Glam. This is Singapore's old Malay district, (5) **and / or** is now a popular shopping destination. Chinatown is popular with residents and tourists, (6) **but / so** it can get crowded, (7) **but / or** it's a fun place.

If you want a nice carpet, head to Little India, (8) **so / or** go over to Arab Street. Both neighborhoods are great places for bargains. Further out from downtown, the East Coast is mostly residential, (9) **so / but** it has many kilometers of beautiful beaches, (10) **or / so** is worth a trip out. Singapore's neighborhoods really do have something for everyone.

---

2 Combine these sentences. Use the correct conjunctions.

1 The signs in Singapore are in English. It is easy to get around.

2 There is a park in my neighborhood. No one goes there.

3 You can easily get a taxi on the street. It is easy to call for a taxi.

4 I have a lot of friends in my neighborhood. They all live nearby.

Grammar

THE PRESENT PROGRESSIVE TENSE

The present progressive tense is used to talk about actions happening now. It is also used to talk about longer actions that are happening around now and will continue in the future. Study the form:

Form	Example
subject + *am / is / are* + present participle (*-ing*)	I am studying at the library right now.
	About 85% of the population is living in high-rise public housing units.
	Singapore is working toward being a global leader in Information Technology.
	More and more people are moving to Singapore to work.

1 Complete this paragraph. Use the present progressive tense of the verbs in the box.

buy	change	invest	make
pay	push	shop	start

I love my neighborhood, and it (1) _____ really fast right now. More and more young people (2) _____ older homes. They (3) _____ a lot of money to fix them up, but unfortunately, that (4) _____ up the rent prices. I (5) _____ about $800 in rent now. I think that's enough. It (6) _____ the sidewalks more crowded as well. However, there are some good things about all this. Some interesting cafés and shops (7) _____ to open. I like the new café near my house. It's a Lebanese place called *Meze*. A lot more people (8) _____ in the stores in our neighborhood, rather than going elsewhere.

2 Circle the correct verb tenses in bold.

1 a A lot of shops **close / are closing** these days.

   b I **know / am knowing** business is terrible.

2 a A lot of people **begin / are beginning** to move into our neighborhood.

   b That's great. My friend Jill **wants / is wanting** to move over here, too.

3 a Paul **takes / is taking** five classes this semester.

   b Really? He **needs / is needing** to slow down.

4 a We **plan / are planning** a trip to Singapore.

   b How nice. **Do you save / Are you saving** up your money?

WRITING TASK

Read this paragraph. <u>Underline</u> the verbs in the present progressive tense.
Circle the conjunctions that link compound sentences.

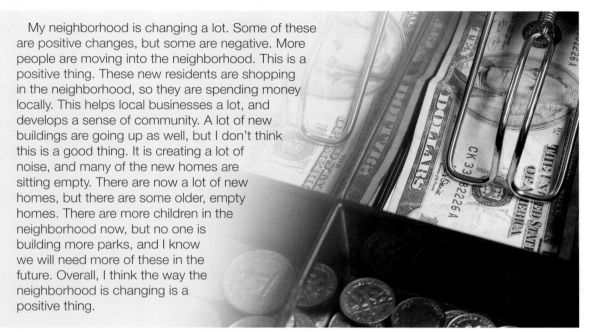

My neighborhood is changing a lot. Some of these are positive changes, but some are negative. More people are moving into the neighborhood. This is a positive thing. These new residents are shopping in the neighborhood, so they are spending money locally. This helps local businesses a lot, and develops a sense of community. A lot of new buildings are going up as well, but I don't think this is a good thing. It is creating a lot of noise, and many of the new homes are sitting empty. There are now a lot of new homes, but there are some older, empty homes. There are more children in the neighborhood now, but no one is building more parks, and I know we will need more of these in the future. Overall, I think the way the neighborhood is changing is a positive thing.

BRAINSTORM

How is your neighborhood changing? Complete the table with your ideas.

How my neighborhood is changing		
Positive changes	**Negative changes**	**Effects**

PLAN

Plan a paragraph describing how your neighborhood is changing. Look back at your brainstorm and write a topic sentence. Decide how you want to organize your paragraph.

WRITE

Write your paragraph. Link some of your sentences with *and, but, or,* or *so.* Pay attention to your use of the present progressive tense.

SHARE

Exchange paragraphs with a partner. Look at the checklist on page 109 and provide feedback to your partner.

REWRITE AND EDIT

Consider your partner's comments and rewrite your paragraph.

STUDY SKILLS Process writing

Getting started

Discuss these questions with a partner.

1 When you do a writing assignment, what is the first thing you do?
2 What is the last thing you do when writing an assignment?
3 What are the easiest and more difficult things for you when you write?

Scenario

Read this scenario. Think about what Chen did right and what he did wrong.

Consider it

Read these six steps in the writing process. Discuss each one with a partner. What steps did Chen do?

1 **Pre-writing** This is everything you do before you actually write. First you decide on a topic. Next you expand on your topic by brainstorming. After you get your ideas on paper, you then plan your writing. Decide what you will use from your brainstorm and how you will organize the writing.
2 **Writing** Find a quiet place with no distractions. Look over your ideas and start your first draft. If you get stuck take a break but it is important to get the draft on paper. After you have your draft down, look it over to further shape your draft.
3 **Sharing** Share your draft with a teacher or one or more students. Get honest feedback on what works well, and what areas can be improved.
4 **Revising** After you consider the feedback, decide what big changes to make. You might choose to add, rearrange, remove, or replace information. Then revise your draft.
5 **Editing** Once you revise your draft, edit it by going through it line by line. Make sure each sentence is as strong as it can be. Focus on word choice, grammar, sentence clarity, spelling, and punctuation.
6 **Submission** In this stage you finalize your writing and share it with a wider audience.

Chen just did his writing homework. His teacher gave him a choice of topics and he chose one. Then he went to his study space and thought about what he would write. Next he wrote his first draft on his computer. He then showed it to a classmate and got feedback. At the same time he read his classmate's paper and gave feedback. He considered the feedback he got and made changes to his draft. In some cases he added information, in some cases he cut information, and in other cases he reordered ideas. Chen then gave the paper to his teacher.

Over to you

Discuss these questions with a partner.

1 Do you think pre-writing is a necessary step? Why or why not?
2 What could happen if you edit before revising?
3 With the use of computers, is the editing step still necessary? Why or why not?

Patterns

Discussion point

Discuss these questions with a partner.

1 Describe the pattern of the flower farm in the picture.

   The picture shows a pattern which is ...

2 Look around. What patterns do you see?

   I can see many patterns. They are ...

3 What patterns can you find in your behavior?

   I always ...

READING	Determining main ideas and supporting details Taking notes
VOCABULARY	Adding prefixes for negation
WRITING	Using end punctuation and capitalization
GRAMMAR	Giving advice and making suggestions

Vocabulary preview

In each set, match the words with their meanings.

1	assume	___	**a**	as good as you can imagine
2	gradually	___	**b**	to believe something to be true, even with no proof
3	ideal	___	**c**	slowly and in small stages
4	in common	___	**d**	to have the same features as something else
5	maximum	___	**e**	to happen again
6	recur	___	**f**	a set of things arranged in a particular order
7	sequence	___	**g**	the largest number or amount possible

READING 1 Time for a change

Before you read

Look at the picture. What bad habit do you see? Why do you think people develop bad habits? Do you have any of the bad habits in the box on the right? Discuss with a partner.

The person in the picture is … . I think people develop bad habits because …
I do have a bad habit. Sometimes, I …

Global reading

Skim *Time for a change*. Check (✓) what it is about.

1 ☐ Why we fail to make changes.   3 ☐ Reasons we develop bad habits.
2 ☐ Ideas for breaking bad habits.   4 ☐ How to develop good study habits.

Close reading

> **DETERMINING MAIN IDEAS AND SUPPORTING DETAILS**
>
> It is essential that you are able to recognize the main idea in a paragraph. The main idea is the most important idea and is located in the topic sentence. To determine the main idea, ask yourself, "What point is the author trying to make?"
>
> Other sentences support the main idea. Identifying these supporting details allows you to make sense of the main idea.

1 Read *Time for a change*. Decide which is the main idea and supporting detail in each paragraph. Write *M* (main idea) or *S* (supporting detail).

1 **a** You need to decide that you want to change and commit yourself to making the change.   ___
  b It is also helpful to talk to people around you.   ___
2 **a** You should try to figure out what is causing the bad habit to recur.   ___
  b Maybe you are late because you like the attention you receive when you arrive late.   ___
3 **a** Then set a goal for change, but you have to set a realistic one.   ___
  b You didn't develop your bad habit overnight, so don't expect to break it overnight.   ___
4 **a** You will need to monitor yourself and track your progress.   ___
  b Keep a journal or diary, or just write things in a notebook.   ___
5 **a** Reward yourself for good behavior!   ___
  b You shouldn't reward yourself by skipping exercise the next week.   ___

BAD HABITS

being late for class
being lazy
biting your nails
eating unhealthy food
skipping appointments
spending too much money

2 **Decide where these sentences go in *Time for a change*. Write the letters in the boxes in the text.**

a You can always adjust your goal to push yourself more later.

b Decide what the next week's reward might be and keep that in mind if you feel you might slip.

c The important thing is to get back on track as quickly as possible.

d Your true friends will support you and help you stay committed.

e If you like the feeling you get when you buy something, for example, look for ways to reproduce the feeling, in a more positive way.

ACADEMIC KEYWORDS		
attention	(n)	/əˈtenʃ(ə)n/
improve	(v)	/ɪmˈpruv/
progress	(n)	/ˈprɑgrəs/

Time for a change

Life coach Jared Price is our featured contributor this week. Jared explains that breaking those recurring bad habits is not as hard as you might think.

Good habit   Bad habit

¹ Let's assume that you already know what bad habit you want to change. Maybe you are always late, you spend too much time online, or you shop even when you can't afford to. To break any habit, what's the first thing you need to do? You need to decide that you want to change and commit yourself to making the change. How can you do this? First, it's important to be honest with yourself about your bad habit. It's also helpful to talk to people around you. Ask them to point out every time they notice your bad habit. Ask for their help and encouragement. There's an old saying—"The best mirror is an old friend." (1) ☐

² After you decide to make a change, look at yourself. You should try to figure out what is causing the bad habit to recur. Maybe you are late because you like the attention you receive when you arrive late. Or perhaps you want to control others by setting the time. Knowledge is power—after you know the reasons behind a bad habit, you can take the step toward breaking it. (2) ☐

³ Then set a goal for change, but you have to set a realistic one. You didn't develop your bad habit overnight, so don't expect to break it overnight. For instance, if you want to lose weight, don't cut out all the things you love to eat. Instead, simply eat less of them or eat them less frequently. If your goal is to get into great shape and you currently do no exercise, don't expect to suddenly start spending two hours at the gym each day. Set a goal of exercising a maximum of several days a week at first. (3) ☐

⁴ You will need to monitor yourself and track your progress. Keep a journal or diary, or just write things in a notebook. If your goal is to improve your grades, exercise more, or eat healthier, there are many cell phone apps that can record your progress. Seeing how you are gradually breaking your bad habit will then start to be its own reward. This will motivate you to continue on the road you are taking. It's also important not to get discouraged by the occasional slip. (4) ☐

⁵ So let's say you exercised all week. Reward yourself for good behavior! You shouldn't reward yourself by skipping exercise the next week or celebrating with a big dinner. Instead, get out with some good friends or buy that jacket you really want. We all react well to praise or positive reinforcement. (5) ☐

Developing critical thinking

Discuss these questions in a group.

1 Which of the bad study habits in the box on the right are difficult to break?

... is very easy / difficult to break, because ...

2 What other suggestions for breaking a bad habit might be useful?

Another suggestion for breaking a bad study habit might be to ...

3 What examples of positive reinforcement that a teacher might use can you name? Do you react well to positive reinforcement?

Positive reinforcement makes me study harder / less hard because ...

BAD STUDY HABITS
cramming
having disorganized notes
not studying enough
skipping class
talking in class

READING 2 The Fibonacci sequence

Before you read

Look at these pictures. What do they have in common? Discuss with a partner.

The pictures all show ...

Global reading

Skim *The Fibonacci sequence*. Check (✓) the best subtitle.

1 ☐ An Italian mathematician

2 ☐ Nature's numbering system

3 ☐ How many rabbits?

Close reading

1 Highlight and/or annotate *The Fibonacci sequence*.

> **▌ TAKING NOTES**
>
> In addition to highlighting and annotating (unit 3), you can take detailed notes after you have read a text more closely. Study these techniques:
> - Write the title and date to help you organize your notes later.
> - Look at the highlighted and annotated text to note the most important information.
> - Use cards, a notebook, or paper that can be inserted into a binder.
> - Use symbols, abbreviations, charts, and colors.
> - Do not copy word for word unless it is a quotation. Use your own words.
> - Review your notes after you complete them. Add your own thoughts.

2 Read these notes from the first two paragraphs of *The Fibonacci sequence*. Take notes on the rest of the text. Then compare your notes with a partner.

> *The Fibonacci sequence*   *Sept. 24*
>
> *FS = recurring math pattern*
> - *in many plants & animals, e.g. pineapple, sunflower, fern, pinecone, shell*
> - *named after math. L. Fibonacci (Italy, 13th cent.)*
> - *didn't discover, but used as ex. in book.*

3 Read the sentences about the Fibonacci sequence. Write *T* (true) or *F* (false). Then correct the false sentences.

1 Leonardo Fibonacci discovered the Fibonacci number sequence. ___

2 Each number in the sequence is the sum of the previous three numbers. ___

3 The final number in the Fibonacci sequence is 987. ___

4 The sequence is used to show that some plants grow efficiently. ___

5 The Fibonacci sequence can be seen in modern, but not old, buildings. ___

THE *F*IBONACCI SEQUENCE

Month	Number of adult pairs	Number of pairs of babies born	Total pairs
January	1	0	1
February	1	1	2
March	2	1	3
April	3	2	5
May	5	3	8
June	8	5	13
July	13	8	21
August	21	13	34
September	34	21	55
October	55	34	89
November	89	55	144
December	144	89	233
January	233	144	377

The number of adult rabbit pairs living each month shows the Fibonacci sequence: 1, 1, 2, 3, 5, 13, etc.

[1] What do a pineapple, a sunflower, and a fern have in common? At first you might think very little, but they are all examples of recurring patterns in nature. These plants, as well as pinecones, seashells, and many other plants and animal species, are linked by a mathematical sequence of numbers called the Fibonacci sequence.

[2] The sequence is named after Leonardo Fibonacci, a thirteenth-century Italian mathematician. He did not discover the sequence, but used it as an example in one of his books.

[3] The sequence consists of numbers, like this: 0, 1, 1, 2, 3, 5, 8, 13, 21, 34, 55, 89, 144, 233, 377, 610, etc. As you can see, starting with 0 and 1, each number is the sum of the previous two numbers: zero plus one equals one, one plus one equals two, one plus two equals three, and so on.

[4] The numbers can describe, for example, the placement of the seeds in a sunflower. The spirals alternate in opposite directions. This allows a large number of seeds to grow efficiently in a small area. This also allows maximum exposure to moisture, light, and air. Of course the plant does not actually use the sequence. It simply grows in the most efficient way possible.

[5] Fibonacci investigated the sequence by setting up a thought experiment about rabbits. Starting with one pair of rabbits, he wanted to know how many pairs of rabbits there would be at the beginning of each month under these circumstances:

- Rabbits are able to reproduce after two months.
- A female rabbit gives birth to a pair of rabbits each month.
- The female rabbit always gives birth to one male and one female rabbit.

[6] The chart shows how many pairs there would be after a year. The Fibonacci sequence gradually emerges in the column "Number of adult pairs."

[7] But the sequence can explain more than rabbit breeding. It can be seen all around us, and not just in plants, animals, and shells. One area where people have used the Fibonacci sequence in daily life is architecture. The numbers of the sequence and their ratios are in structures as old as the Taj Mahal in India.

[8] Modern designers have made use of them as well. An education center called "The Core" is part of a popular visitor attraction in England which has the largest greenhouses in the world. The original design of The Core's ceiling is based on the Fibonacci sequence. By imitating forms found in nature, they made a connection between the building and plants. This is ideal because that is what the attraction is all about.

[9] The world around us is not as random as we might assume. From the seeds in a sunflower to modern architecture, we can find many instances of the Fibonacci sequence.

ACADEMIC KEYWORDS

experiment	(n)	/ɪkˈsperɪment/
link	(v)	/lɪŋk/
original	(adj)	/əˈrɪdʒən(ə)l/

Developing critical thinking

1 Discuss these questions in a group.

1 What number follows in the Fibonacci sequence after 233, 377, and 610?

The next number is ...

2 Some flowers have 8, 13, and 21 petals. Is this because of the Fibonacci sequence?

I think this is / isn't because of the Fibonacci sequence ...

2 Think about the ideas from *Time for a change* and *The Fibonacci sequence* and discuss these questions in a group.

1 Think about the patterns in nature in the box on the right. How do they affect you?

When it's dark and cold, I prefer to ...
Hot weather makes me ...

2 Do you think being efficient is always a good thing? Why or why not?

I think being efficient is always / sometimes / rarely a good thing because ...

PATTERNS IN NATURE	
amount of daylight	tides
seasons	weather

Vocabulary skill

ADDING PREFIXES FOR NEGATION

A prefix is a group of letters added to the beginning of a word to change its meaning.

We can negate some words in English by adding one of these prefixes:

un-	fair → unfair	im-	possible → impossible
dis-	organized → disorganized	il-	logical → illogical
in-	correct → incorrect	ir-	regular → irregular

It is best to consult a dictionary to determine the correct prefix.

1 Add prefixes to these words to make them negative. Then check your dictionary.

1	realistic _____	5	efficient _____	9	personal _____
2	satisfied _____	6	polite _____	10	believable _____
3	popular _____	7	responsible _____	11	legal _____
4	rational _____	8	considerate _____	12	respectful _____

2 Rewrite the second sentences. Use prefixes.

1 I cannot find anything in my room. I am not organized.

2 I cannot do this math problem. It is not possible.

3 Never hack into someone's computer. It is not legal.

4 I do not see any patterns in this number sequence. It is not regular.

5 Are you sure you can achieve that goal? It is not realistic.

6 The correct answer is 11. Your answer is not correct.

7 That does not make any sense. It is not logical.

8 I doubt she can quit eating junk food overnight. It is not likely.

WRITING Giving advice in an email

You are going to learn about end punctuation and capitalization, and expressions for giving advice and making suggestions. You are then going to use these to write an email giving advice.

Writing skill

USING END PUNCTUATION AND CAPITALIZATION

There are three types of end punctuation:

1 A period (.) for statements. *Fibonacci conducted a thought experiment.*

2 A question mark (?) for direct (not indirect) questions. *How many rabbits are there?*

3 An exclamation mark (!) to express strong emotion. *Look out!*

You must capitalize …

- the first word in a sentence: *Set a goal for yourself.*
- names and family words used as names: *Leonardo Fibonacci, Where is Father?*
- titles before names: *Professor Lee*
- proper (specific) nouns: *Golden Gate Bridge*
- days of the week, months, holidays (but not seasons): *Friday, June, Ramadan*
- countries, cities, nationalities, languages: *Brazil, São Paulo, Brazilian*
- direction words with the name of a place: *South Africa*
- content words in titles: *A Tale of Two Cities*

1 **Complete the sentences with end punctuation.**

1 a Guess what___ I solved this math problem—finally___ I hope it's correct___

   b Congratulations___ I know math is not your favorite subject___

2 a Did you hear about Maggie___ She cut up all her credit cards___

   b She did___ I knew she wanted to change some of her shopping habits___

3 a Quick___ Look over there___

   b That's amazing___ But what, exactly, is it___

2 **Add capital letters to these sentences.**

1 the fibonacci numbers can be seen in the taj mahal in india.

2 please ask mother and father what time dinner is.

3 today is tuesday, april 13.

4 is the test on monday or tuesday?

5 my favorite book is *of mice and men*.

6 venezuela is a country in the northern part of south america.

7 omar speaks english, arabic, and french.

8 drive west until you get to the town of east dayton.

9 mr. and mrs. peterson moved to new york city last summer.

10 the red sea separates east africa from the arabian peninsula.

Grammar

GIVING ADVICE AND MAKING SUGGESTIONS

To give advice, you can use the modal verbs *should / should not*. You can also use the verbs *need to* and *have to* to give advice. These are stronger than *should*. Study the forms:

Form	Example
should / should not subject + *should / should not* + base form	You should identify the bad habit. He should not get discouraged.
need to *I / You / We / They + need to +* base form *He / She / It + needs to +* base form	You need to track your progress. He needs to track his progress.
have to *I / You / We / They + have to +* base form *He / She / It + has to +* base form	You have to set a realistic goal. He has to set a realistic goal.

You can make suggestions with adjective + infinitive form expressions:

Form	Example
It is + adjective + *to* + base form	It is good to reward yourself. It is important to be honest. It is ideal to talk to other people. It is not good to expect change overnight.

1 Rewrite these sentences giving advice for saving money. Use the words in parentheses.

1 Make shopping lists. (it is good to)
2 Buy things on sale. (should)
3 Do not eat out so much. (should not)
4 Take public transportation (it is important to)
5 Open a savings account. (have to)
6 Keep a budget. (need to)
7 Be careful with your credit cards. (should)
8 Do not buy designer goods. (It is not good to)

2 Correct these sentences about writing an email.

1 You needs to address the person first.
2 You should to include a clear subject line.
3 It is a good to keep things short and simple.
4 It is important remember that emails are permanent.
5 It is ideal to should answer email right away.
6 You should not wrote things you would not say.
7 You should checking the email before you send it.
8 It not good to type in capital letters.

WRITING TASK

Read this email.  the modals and expressions that give advice. Correct the capitalization or end punctuation errors.

To: Terry@email.com

Subject: my advice

Hi terry,

I got your email last saturday asking me for my advice about studying in london. First, congratulations. I'm happy you got accepted. My Summer program there was great. Are you also planning to start the program in july.

There are some excellent professors there? You should write to professor Radison. She can help answer some questions, too. I will send you her email. They have a booklet for new students called "Tips for new Students" and I'm sure she will send you that!

It's good to arrive early so you can get settled before classes start. It's important to reserve an early place if you want to live in the dorms? You need to apply for a place before march. You shouldn't worry, though. I think there is plenty of time! Or are you going to rent an apartment.

I'm really glad I can help. Write me back with specific questions!

Robin

BRAINSTORM

Your friend needs advice on one of the topics in the box. Choose one topic and complete the table with your ideas.

| how to break a bad habit   how to develop better study habits |
| how to get into an overseas graduate school   how to improve his or her academic vocabulary |

Things to do	Things not to do

PLAN

Plan an email giving advice. Discuss other possible ideas with your partner. Then choose at least four of the best ideas to include.

WRITE

Write your email. Pay attention to your use of *should / should not* and other verbs and expressions that give advice.

SHARE

Exchange emails with your partner. Look at the checklist on page 109 and provide feedback to your partner.

REWRITE AND EDIT

Consider your partner's comments and rewrite your email. Pay attention to your end punctuation and use of capitalization.

Where does the time go?

by Stella Cottrell

If you are not sure where your time goes, for a few days write in your diary everything you do – roughly every hour. Be as accurate as you can – nobody will see this except you!

Work out approximately how many hours each day you spend on sleep, exercise, lectures, etc. Draw a time circle, like the ones below, and divide it into a 24-hour day.

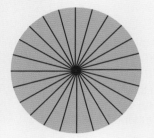

Circle 1: How I use time now

Using different colors or symbols for each type of activity, mark in where your time usually goes in a day. Treat each section as roughly one hour.

Which activities are left out or do not receive enough time? Which activities take up too much time?

Example

- sleep – 10 hr
- eating – 2 hr
- socializing – 3 hr
- personal/home – 3 hr
- travel – 1 hr
- lectures, seminars, tutorials – 2 hr
- reading – 2 hr
- writing – 1 hr
- thinking – 0 hr
- exercise/relaxation – 0 hr

Circle 2: How I want to use my time

Draw another time circle. Divide the day into how you would prefer to use your time so that your day is balanced between different activities. This is your goal to work towards.

Example

- sleep – 8 hr
- eating and socializing – 3 hr
- personal/home – 2 hr
- travel – 1 hr
- lectures, seminars, tutorials – 2 hr
- reading – 3 1/2 hr
- writing – 2 hr
- thinking – 1 hr
- exercise/relaxation – 1 1/2 hr

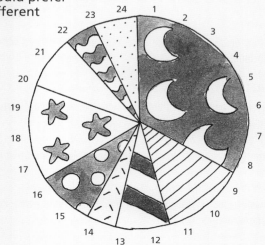

Speed

READING	Distinguishing facts from opinions Identifying tone
VOCABULARY	Organizing new words: adjectives and adverbs
WRITING	Using commas and colons
GRAMMAR	Comparative forms of adjectives and adverbs

Discussion point

Discuss these questions with a partner.

1 Do you think the animals in the picture are moving quickly or slowly? Why?

I think they're moving ... because ...

2 What is something that most people in your country do slowly?

People in my country ... slowly.

3 What is something that most people in your country do quickly?

People in my country ... quickly.

Vocabulary preview

Complete these sentences. Use the words in the box.

| advocate | appeal | associate | emphasized |
| functional | impact | origin | pace |

1 After my crazy week, a quiet weekend has an _____ to it.

2 The beneficial _____ of exercise on weight loss is well-known.

3 The winner ran at a steady _____—not too fast or too slow.

4 What do you _____ the word "quick" with?

5 The _____ of skiing can be traced back to Scandinavia.

6 My personal trainer _____ that I need to set clear goals.

7 She is an _____ of doing things slowly, but thoroughly.

8 The new high-speed trains are _____, not comfortable.

READING 1 Hurry up and slow down!

Before you read

1 **Do you do the actions in the box on the right quickly, slowly, or at an average speed? Discuss with a partner.**

I ... very quickly, but I ... very slowly. I ... at an average speed.

2 **Preview *Hurry up and slow down!* Check (✓) your predictions for what topics are discussed.**

1 ☐ Who the movement attracts   **3** ☐ The future of the movement

2 ☐ How the movement started   **4** ☐ How the movement's ideas spread

ACTIONS

eat	wake up
fall asleep	walk
read	write
talk	

Global reading

Skim *Hurry up and slow down!* Check your predictions.

Close reading

1 **Read *Hurry up and slow down!* Check (✓) the interviewer's purpose.**

1 ☐ inform   **2** ☐ entertain   **3** ☐ persuade

DISTINGUISHING FACTS FROM OPINIONS

A text may contain both facts and opinions, so you need to know the difference between them. A fact expresses a truth. An opinion expresses a belief, feeling, or judgment. It may be based on facts, but it cannot be proven. Read carefully to determine if someone is expressing a fact or opinion.

---

2 **Read these sentences from *Hurry up and slow down!* Write *F* (fact) or *O* (opinion).**

1 It's best to live your life slowly. _____

2 The word *slow* should be redefined. _____

3 There is no single member's profile. _____

4 It's better to emphasize quality, not quantity. _____

5 There is more to life than increasing its speed. _____

Hurry up & slow down!

Roberto Perez, an advocate of the Slow Movement, talks to *Living Life*.

¹ What does the Slow Movement believe?

It's best to live your life slowly. The word "slow" should be redefined. It needs to be more positive. Right now it is associated with failure, as in "slow progress." We hope others join our movement.

² When did you become a member?

It was in 2006, the day after I was late for my daughter's graduation. I went to the office to do some work that morning and got stuck in traffic. After that I knew I wanted a slower, simpler, richer life.

³ What is a typical member like?

There is no single member's profile. We are many things: doctors, farmers, students, and chefs. However, we always give the same reasons for our inability to slow down. We travel further to get to work. We work longer hours. We are connected 24/7. The need for speed is the worst thing in people's lives. It destroys our health, families, and communities. It's better to emphasize quality, not quantity. Gandhi once said, "There is more to life than increasing its speed." We want everyone to believe this.

⁴ What are the origins of the movement?

It all began with food. In 1986, a journalist called Carlo Petrini witnessed the opening of an American fast-food restaurant in an old part of Rome. He understood the dangers to local traditions and dietary habits. He was especially concerned that people would eat cheap, unhealthy food. The Slow Food Movement was created to protect local food against the dangers of fast-food culture.

⁵ I see. And did it spread quickly?

No. True to itself, it spread slowly. The movement now has 83,000 members in more than 130 countries. After the Slow Food Movement, the idea spread to other areas. One of the most popular is the Slow Travel Movement. Followers look for more relaxed ways to travel that have a lower impact on the environment. Other "slow" movements include the Slow Design Movement and Slow Parenting Movement.

⁶ What is the Slow Internet Movement?

Oh, that was a kind of joke. It happened on April Fool's Day, or the first of April. In the U.S., that's a day when people play tricks on each other. Anyway, on April 1, 2011, a radio station did a story on a movement to slow down the Internet. It discussed internet cafés with slow internet connections, where people would spend hours drinking coffee and checking email. A scientist said that our perception of time would change if the Internet were slower. For example, a photo that takes a minute to download would feel like four minutes, and so our lives would feel longer. Our lives wouldn't be longer of course—they would just seem it. What's interesting is that the story was false, but many believed it.

⁷ Interesting. Why do you think they believed it?

Although many demand faster and faster internet connections, I think there was an appeal to what the story suggested: A slower and more relaxed pace of life, that is less functional and more enjoyable.

⁸ I can understand that appeal! Thank you, Roberto, for talking with us today.

You're very welcome.

Developing critical thinking

Discuss these questions in a group.

1 Read the reasons why people slow down in the box on the right. Do you think slowing down would lead to these things? Why or why not?

   I think that slowing down would / wouldn't lead to ... because ...

2 What would you find challenging about slowing down your life?

   If I had to slow down my life, I would find ... very challenging.

3 Do you think slowing down the Internet would increase or decrease stress?

   Slowing down the Internet would cause me more / less stress because ...

REASONS FOR SLOWING DOWN

better appreciation of things
better health
closer friendships
less stress
more relaxed lifestyle
more time

READING 2 Keeping up with the Tarahumara

Before you read

Which of the ways of getting around in the box on the right do you use? Why? What do you think is the best way to get around? Discuss with a partner.

Usually, I get around by ... because ...
I never get around by ... because...
I think the best way to get around is ... because ...

WAYS OF GETTING AROUND	
bicycle	subway
bus	taxi
car	train
moped	walking

Global reading

Skim *Keeping up with the Tarahumara*. Check (✓) what the text is mainly about.

1 ☐ Famous running races that the Tarahumara have participated in

2 ☐ The tradition of long-distance running among the Tarahumara

3 ☐ Why the Tarahumara have abandoned running in modern times

Close reading

IDENTIFYING TONE

The tone of a text is the attitude or opinion that the author takes toward the subject. Possible tones include: humorous or dry, serious or light-hearted, and supportive or unsupportive. As you read, notice the specific words that the author chooses to help you determine the tone.

1 **Read *Keeping up with the Tarahumara*. Check (✓) the author's tone.**

  1 ☐ humorous   3 ☐ unsupportive   5 ☐ doubtful
  2 ☐ admiring   4 ☐ pessimistic

2 **Compare your answer with a partner. What words from the text helped you determine your answer?**

3 **Write the answers to these questions.**

  1 Where in Mexico do the Tarahumara live?
  2 What does *Rarámuri* mean?
  3 Which is bigger: a *rancho* or a *pueblo*?
  4 What are two crops that the Tarahumara grow?
  5 How long are their running courses?
  6 What place did Victoriano get in the ultra-marathon?

4 **Check (✓) the statements you can infer from *Keeping up with the Tarahumara***

  1 ☐ Some Tarahumara run between pueblos.
  2 ☐ The Tarahumara live in an isolated part of Mexico.
  3 ☐ The goats, cows, and sheep that they raise do not taste good.
  4 ☐ A rabbit and a deer run at the same speed.
  5 ☐ Children help raise the animals.
  6 ☐ The Tarahumara do not rely on motorized transportation.
  7 ☐ Tarahumara women do not like competing in races.
  8 ☐ The Tarahumara have a lot of foot problems when they are old.

Keeping up with the
TARAHUMARA

[1] A lone young man runs barefoot through the pink glow of the rising sun. He runs effortlessly down a narrow trail at a steady pace. Remarkably, he has run nearly 100 kilometers. However, he has only stopped a couple of times for water. He still has many, many kilometers to run. This is not a problem. He will continue to run for several more hours. This young man is a Tarahumara Indian.

[2] Tarahumara runners emphasize distance over speed. They live in the canyon country of northern Mexico. The Tarahumara name probably comes from a Spanish version of the name they call themselves, *Rarámuri*, which means "foot runner." They live in groups of households called *ranchos*. There are between two and twenty-five houses in each rancho, with each rancho between one and eight kilometers apart. An area of about twenty-four kilometers forms a geographical and political unit called a *pueblo*. It is because of these large distances between pueblos that the Tarahumara have become such good runners.

[3] There are traditional reasons for running, but there are also functional reasons. The Tarahumara grow corn, beans, and other crops, and raise animals such as goats, cows, and sheep, but they rarely use them for food. In the past, when they wanted meat, they would simply chase a rabbit or a deer. They would run very, very long distances and eventually tire the animal to the point when they could, incredibly, catch it.

[4] Running becomes a way of life early for these people. Children start running early, chasing sheep and goats to keep them from wandering too far away. Runners are often sent between pueblos to deliver news or goods, and groups travel long distances to attend ceremonies. The quickest way to travel is simply to run.

[5] The Tarahumara regularly hold races between neighboring pueblos. A running course may be anywhere between 48 and 160 kilometers long. In addition to running, the runners sometimes move a wooden ball along the entire length of the race using only their feet. The women also compete in some races. They throw and catch round hoops while running.

[6] The Tarahumara are famous in the running world. Three Tarahumara entered an ultra-marathon in the U.S. when they were promised food to feed their pueblos. Victoriano, a 55-year-old man, won the race. Another man from his pueblo named Cirrildo won second place. The third Tarahumara runner, Manuel Luna, placed fifth.

[7] The Tarahumara, with their long and proud tradition of running, have provided some of the best runners in the world. From simple origins, they are admired as world-class athletes. For many professional runners, there is an appeal to the Tarahumara method of running, and more and more people are becoming advocates of barefoot running.

Tarahumara live here

ACADEMIC KEYWORDS		
attend	(v)	/əˈtend/
method	(n)	/ˈmeθəd/
provide	(v)	/prəˈvaɪd/

Developing critical thinking

1 Discuss these questions in a group.

   1 How well do you think Tarahumara runners would do in a 100-meter race?

   I think they would be quick / slow in a 100-meter race because ...

   2 Do you think the number of Tarahumara runners is increasing or decreasing? Why? Think about the things in the box on the right.

   I think the number of runners is increasing / decreasing because ...

THINK ABOUT:	
family	money
jobs	resources
media attention	transportation

2 **Think about the ideas from *Hurry up and slow down!* and *Keeping up with the Tarahumara* and discuss these questions in a group.**

1 Which of the characteristics in the box on the right do you think the Tarahumara would use to describe the Slow Movement?

The Tarahumara would describe the Slow Movement as ... because ...

2 How do you think members of the Slow Movement would describe the Tarahumara way of life?

The Slow Movement might describe the Tarahumara way of life as ...

CHARACTERISTICS	
difficult	modern
healthy	spoiled
interesting	strange
lazy	traditional

Vocabulary skill

ORGANIZING NEW WORDS: ADJECTIVES AND ADVERBS

Besides nouns and verbs (unit 2), two of the most common parts of speech are adjectives and adverbs.

<u>Adjectives</u> describe nouns. They usually appear before nouns or after the verb *be*.

*He understood the dangers to **local** traditions and **dietary** habits.*

*The news story was **false**.*

<u>Adverbs</u> describe how, when, how often, or where a verb happened.

*It's best to live your life **slowly**.* (how?)

*We hope others join our movement **soon**.* (when?)

*We **always** cite the same reasons for our inability to slow down.* (how often?)

*I have never been **there**.* (where?)

1 **Read these sentences from *Keeping up with the Tarahumara*. Write *ADJ* (adjective) or *ADV* (adverb) for the words in bold.**

1 He runs **effortlessly** down a narrow trail at a steady pace. _____

2 There are **traditional** reasons for running. _____

3 They **rarely** use them for food. _____

4 They would run very, very **long** distances. _____

5 Children start running **early**. _____

6 The **quickest** way to travel is simply to run. _____

7 The runners sometimes move a **wooden** ball. _____

8 They are admired as **world-class** athletes. _____

2 **Complete the sentences. Use the adjectives and adverbs in the box.**

careful	comfortable	famous	now
quickly	slow	sometimes	there

1 I _____ go jogging before I go to school.

2 I am going to stop _____. I cannot go on.

3 Please be _____. These steps are uneven.

4 Rex is a _____ walker. What takes him so long?

5 These tennis shoes are not _____. I'm going to return them.

6 I would love to visit Mexico. Have you ever been _____?

7 There are a lot of _____ long-distance runners from Kenya.

8 Can you drive _____? I am in a hurry.

WRITING Making a comparison

You are going to learn about commas and colons, and the comparative forms of adjectives and adverbs. You are then going to use these to write a paragraph making a comparison.

Writing skill

USING COMMAS AND COLONS

Use a comma …

- to separate three or more items: *The Tarahumara grow corn, beans, and other crops.*
- after an introductory phrase: *True to itself, it spread slowly.*
- to rename something: *Victoriano, a 55-year-old man, won the race.*
- after a dependent clauses: *Before he finished, he stopped for water.*
- to separate clauses with different subjects: *You run fast, but I don't.*
- to introduce a quotation: *Gandhi said, "There is more to life than increasing its speed."*

Use a colon …

- to introduce a list: *We are many things: doctors, farmers, students, and, chefs.*
- to emphasize a word or phrase: *Athletes know the Tarahumara for one thing: running.*

1 Read these sentences. Correct the comma and colon mistakes.

1 You will need to bring three things, a notebook, pens, and a calculator.
2 A lot of people like to travel at high speeds: but I hate it.
3 Like many people: I have an online profile.
4 She works all day. In addition: she takes classes at night.
5 If I can give you one piece of advice it is this, exercise.
6 Before you start running: it is good to do a 15-minutes warm-up.
7 I love to run: but my friends hate to run.
8 My father always says "Slow down! No one is going to take your food away."

2 Complete this paragraph with commas and colons.

Since its formation the Slow Food Movement has been an international organization that promotes food culture as an alternative to fast food. It has these aims encourage farming preserve food traditions and protect cultivation techniques. It was established as part of the Slow Movement. However it has since grown as a movement in its own right. There are offices in eight countries Italy Germany Switzerland the U.S.A. France Japan Chile and the U.K. Carlo Petrini its founder is still active in the movement. To spread the message to a younger generation volunteers teach gardening skills to students.

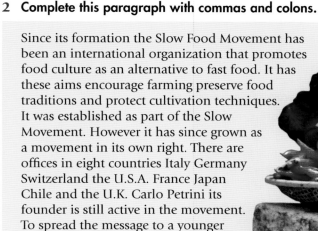

Grammar

COMPARATIVE FORMS OF ADJECTIVES AND ADVERBS

We use the comparative form of adjectives and adverbs to point out how two things are different. Study the forms:

Form	Example
One syllable adjectives and adverbs not ending in -e or vowel + consonant *adjective / adverb + -er*	old → older
One syllable adjectives and adverbs ending in -e *adjective / adverb + -r*	safe → safer
One syllable adjectives and adverbs ending in vowel + consonant *adjective / adverb + consonant + -er*	big → bigger
Two syllable adjectives ending in -y *(adjective / adverb -y) + -ier*	pretty → prettier
Two or more syllable adjectives not ending in -y *more + adjective*	modern → more modern
Two or more syllable <u>adverbs</u> ending in -ly *more + adverb*	quickly → more quickly
You must memorize irregular adjectives and adverbs.	good / well → better bad / badly → worse far → farther / further

We use *than* to make comparisons.

*Your car is faster **than** mine.*   *You walk more slowly **than** I do.*

1 Write the comparative forms of these words.

Adjectives	Adverbs	Adjectives or adverbs
1 easy _____	6 noisily _____	10 slow _____
2 famous _____	7 easily _____	11 fast _____
3 big _____	8 badly _____	12 far _____
4 good _____	9 well _____	
5 wide _____		

2 Combine these sentences. Use the comparative form of the words in parentheses.

1 Lions can run 80 kilometers an hour. Horses can run 77 kilometers an hour. (fast)
   Lions can run faster than horses.

2 Tom ran the race in 45 minutes. Joe ran the race in 55 minutes. (quickly)

3 Noor travels a kilometer to school. Oscar travels five kilometers to school. (far)

4 Beth's grade on the exam was a C. Alex's grade on the exam was an A-. (bad)

5 It is 25 degrees Celsius in Chicago. It is 22 degrees Celsius in New York. (hot)

6 Kenzo can run for 30 minutes. Tim can run for 50 minutes. (long)

7 Chemistry 101 is easy. Chemistry 103 is not easy at all. (difficult)

8 An airplane ticket costs a lot. A bus ride does not cost a lot. (expensive)

WRITING TASK

Read this paragraph. <u>Underline</u> the comparative adjectives. (Circle) the comparative adverbs. Correct the comma or colon errors.

I shop in both supermarkets and convenience stores. Both have their plusses and minuses: but overall I prefer to shop in convenience stores. Supermarkets are bigger than convenience stores. Therefore: they take longer to get through. I feel they are also more impersonal. There is a lot a choice in a supermarket but I don't need all that choice. The food is fresher in supermarkets than in convenience stores. However: the lines are always longer. I can get though the lines more quickly in a convenience store. Convenience stores often stay open later so are, of course, more convenient. The prices in convenience stores are almost always higher than in supermarkets, but I usually try to buy things on sale. In fact: there are three things I never buy in convenience stores fruit vegetables and meat. If I want them the supermarket is better.

BRAINSTORM

Read the four topics and their factors to compare in the box. Choose one of these topics and write two athletes, cities, gadgets, or stores to compare in the first row of the table. List the factors you will consider in the first column. Make comparisons in the second and third columns with your ideas.

> **athletes** (factors: age, ability, talent, personality)
> **cities** (factors: size, location, weather, shopping)
> **gadgets** (factors: price, weight, age, design)
> **stores** (factors: location. price, size, hours)

	1	2

PLAN

Plan a paragraph comparing two things. Discuss other possible ideas with your partner. Choose at least four ideas to include in your paragraph.

WRITE

Write your comparison. Pay attention to your use of the comparative forms of adjectives and adverbs.

SHARE

Exchange paragraphs with a partner. Look at the checklist on page 109 and provide feedback to your partner.

REWRITE AND EDIT

Consider your partner's comments and rewrite your paragraph. Pay attention to your use of commas and colons.

STUDY SKILLS Keeping a journal

Getting started

Discuss these questions with a partner.

1 Do you like to write about your experiences, thoughts, and feelings? Why or why not?
2 Have you ever kept a journal? If so, what did you write about?
3 Read the reasons many people keep journals. Can you give any other reasons?

It is an opportunity to practice writing.
It is a way to keep a written record of daily events.
You can use your journal in the future for personal reflection.

Scenario

Read this scenario. Think about what Fatima is doing right and what she is doing wrong.

Consider it

Read these five tips for starting a journal. Discuss each one with a partner. Can you give any other tips for journal writing?

1 **Be organized** Use a lined notebook or a blank journal. Write down the date at the top of the page. You may also want to include the time of day and place.
2 **Keep calm** Write wherever you feel relaxed and comfortable.
3 **Be honest** Write from the heart about your feelings, thoughts, and experiences.
4 **Write quickly** Do not be too concerned about spelling, grammar, and punctuation. It is more important to get your ideas on paper.
5 **Write often** You do not have to write every day, but the more you write, the better.

Over to you

Discuss these questions with a partner.

1 How is journal writing different from other types of writing?
2 Is it a good idea to show your journal writing to others? Why or why not?
3 What differences would there be, if any, in keeping a journal on a computer?

Fatima has recently started keeping a journal. She hopes it will help her with her writing in general. She bought a notebook and started writing two weeks ago. She always writes in her study space before she goes to bed. She writes every day, even when she does not want to. She begins by writing the date. She mostly writes about her day and what she felt and thought about. Sometimes she writes questions to herself to think about, and even draws pictures. Fatima writes slowly and carefully, making sure she uses correct grammar, spelling, and punctuation. She has decided that she wants to keep her journal and look at it again in the future.

Vision

READING	Scanning Using a chart to organize your notes
VOCABULARY	Adding suffixes to change verbs into nouns
WRITING	Writing complete sentences
GRAMMAR	Count and noncount nouns

Discussion point

Discuss these questions with a partner.

1 What colors do you see in the picture? Are there any colors you do not see?

I can see a lot of ... . I don't see any ...

2 What is your favorite color? Why?

My favorite color is ... because ...

3 What do you think these idioms mean?

The idiom ... means ...

"to tell a white lie"

"to see things in black and white"

"to see red"

"to do something once in a blue moon"

"to be in a gray area"

"to give someone the green light"

Vocabulary preview

Complete these sentences. Circle **the correct meanings of the words in bold.**

1 The **background** of a picture is _____ the main part.
   a in front of   b behind

2 If you draw a **horizontal** line, you draw it _____ of the page.
   a across the bottom   b down the side

3 When you **perceive** something, you _____ it.
   a notice   b say

4 If you **restrict** something, you _____ it.
   a limit   b expand

5 To **signal** someone, you might _____.
   a move or make a sound   b think about the person

6 If something **symbolizes** something, it _____ it by a sign.
   a defeats   b represents

7 Something **universal** affects _____ in the world.
   a no one   b everyone

8 If you draw a **vertical** line, you draw it _____ of the page.
   a across the bottom   b down the side

READING 1 Is seeing really believing?

Before you read

Try these experiments. Which takes longer? Why? Discuss with a partner.

1 Read the color words as quickly as you can. Time yourself.
2 Say the colors as quickly as you can. Time yourself.

BLUE	YELLOW	ORANGE
GREEN	BLUE	BLUE
PURPLE	GREEN	ORANGE
ORANGE	YELLOW	GREEN
RED	YELLOW	BLUE
PURPLE	PURPLE	RED
RED	RED	PURPLE
BLUE	YELLOW	ORANGE

Global reading

1 **Skim** Is seeing really believing? **Check (✓) what it is mainly about.**

   1 ☐ Color and personality   3 ☐ Number puzzles
   2 ☐ Optical illusions   4 ☐ Web design

> **SCANNING**
>
> Scanning is searching a text to find specific information or key words, such as names, dates, or statistics. Like skimming (unit 2), you do not read every word. You also do not need to start at the beginning of a text. Instead, you can predict where you think the information is and start there.

2 **Scan** Is seeing really believing? Circle **the color words.**

Close reading

Read Is seeing really believing? **Correct these false sentences.**

1 Color is created by our eyes.
2 Illusion plays a role in how our brain perceives images.
3 In the first illusion, the colors are different.
4 Vision is created according to our past experiences.
5 We all see the world in the same way.

IS SEEING REALLY BELIEVING?

🏠 **HOME**   ⚙ **BLOG**   ✆ **CONTACT**

[1] Tomatoes are red, the sky is blue, and bananas are yellow, right? Well, not exactly. Color does not really exist, at least not in a literal or universal sense. What exists is light. Light is real, but color is not. Color is simply created by and restricted to the brain. We know this because colors can look different in our minds.

[2] We're told to trust our eyes, but our eyes just don't have that much to do with vision. We see much more with our brains, and it's easy to play tricks on the brain. We perceive these differences because the brain doesn't necessarily want to see the actual image. Rather, it wants to make sense of the image. The brain does this by looking at the surrounding context.

[3] Look at the two tiles in picture 1. They are identical in color. Now look at what happens when we change their context in picture 2. In their new context, the horizontal and vertical lines look the same, but their colors look different. The context suggests that the dark brown tile on the top shows a poorly reflected surface under bright light. The bright orange tile on the side suggests a highly reflective surface in shadow. You see different colors now because your brain thinks they have a different meaning. This is an example of an optical illusion.

[4] Color is created according to our past experiences. When you see something as an optical illusion, it is because your brain behaves as if the objects in the current images are real, in the same way as images you have seen previously.

[5] Look at the scenes of the desert in picture 3. They have the same color composition of blues and yellows. Now stare at the dot in picture 4 for one minute. Look back at the desert scenes. The reason the colors now appear different is because your brain incorporates the recent history of red on the left and green on the right into the second image, at least for a short time.

[6] This raises the question: Do you see what I see? The answer, in short, is no. Our experiences and histories in the world are different. In fact, none of us even sees the world as it really is, but rather as a meaning derived from our own unique experiences. Seeing is not, in fact, believing.

Developing critical thinking

Discuss these questions in a group.

1 Did the optical illusions work for you? Which was the most interesting?

Both / Neither of the optical illusions worked for me because ...

2 Describe a situation where you "couldn't believe your eyes"?

I couldn't believe my eyes when I saw ...

3 Do you think optical illusions are clever or silly? Why?

In my opinion, optical illusions are clever / silly because ...

ACADEMIC KEYWORDS

derive	(v)	/dɪˈraɪv/
exist	(v)	/ɪɡˈzɪst/
identical	(adj)	/aɪˈdentɪk(ə)l/

READING 2 Colors and flags

Before you read

This pie chart shows the colors on all the countries' flags in the world. What color is most used on the flags? Why do you think this color is used so much? What colors are not very popular? What colors are on your country's flag? Discuss with a partner.

The color that is most used in the pie chart is ... . I think this is because ...
The colors ... are not very popular.
The colors on my country's flag are ...

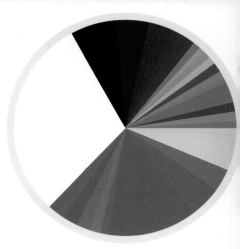

Global reading

Scan *Colors and flags*. Write the country or organization of these flags.

Close reading

1 Highlight and annotate *Colors and flags*, or take notes.

> **USING A CHART TO ORGANIZE YOUR NOTES**
>
> One way to organize the notes you take is to put certain information in charts. This can be especially useful when you are comparing or contrasting information. One of the easiest ways is to organize your notes in columns.

2 Complete the chart about colors in national flags using your annotations or notes. Some colors have two meanings.

	Meaning 1	Meaning 2
Black		
White		
Blue		
Red		
Green		
Yellow		
Red, white, and blue		
Green, gold, and red		
Black, white, green, and red		

3 Complete these sentences.

1 The most common use of flags is to _____.

2 Blue was chosen for the U.N. flag because it is _____.

3 The Olympic™ flag colors were chosen because _____.

4 In motor racing a black and white checked flag means _____.

5 When rules are broken in Canadian football, the _____ flag is used.

1 _____

2 _____

3 _____

4 _____

5 _____

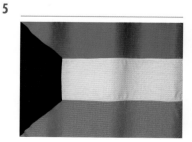

6 _____

Colors and flags

ACADEMIC KEYWORDS

appear	(v)	/əˈpɪr/
indicate	(v)	/ˈɪndɪˌkeɪt/
represent	(v)	/ˌreprɪˈzent/

¹ They decorate, communicate, and warn, but the most common use of flags is to symbolize the unity of a nation. The colors on flags are often highly symbolic as well. Black often represents strength and determination. White can represent peace and purity. Blue can mean freedom and prosperity. Red might represent blood and courage. Green can be the color of earth or agriculture. Yellow or gold often represent the sun and wealth. Of course, with so many countries in the world, individual colors may have different meanings entirely, and may depend on historical or cultural factors, or even how we perceive certain colors.

² Groups of colors can also have meaning. The most common three colors—red, white, and blue—represent freedom and revolution. These colors are on flags from the U.S., the U.K., Chile, Australia, Cuba, and many others. France's flag has three vertical stripes of blue, white, and red, while Russia's has the same colors but with three horizontal stripes. Another popular grouping is green, gold, and red, representing African unity and identity. Mali's flag has three vertical stripes of these colors. Many other African countries also use these three colors, such as Cameroon, Guinea, and Senegal.

³ There are other groupings of colors. For example, Colombia's flag has three vertical stripes. Yellow represents the metal gold, blue represents the sea, and red represents blood. These colors can also be found on the flags of Venezuela and Ecuador, Colombia's neighbors. And then there are the colors that represent Arab unity: black, white, green, and red. Each of these colors represents a different Arab dynasty, or era. The flag of the United Arab Emirates consists of a red vertical stripe on the left side, with three horizontal stripes of green, white, and black. These four colors can be seen on many other flags, including Syria, Kuwait, and Jordan.

⁴ Since 1947, the flag of the United Nations has contained a white world map on a light blue background. These are the official colors of the U.N. Blue was chosen because it is "the opposite of red," which sometimes symbolizes blood. The Olympic™ flag was designed in 1914 and first flown in 1920. It has five rings of blue, yellow, black, green, and red on a white background. These colors were chosen because at least one of them appeared on the flag of every country of the world at that time.

⁵ Flags are used in many sports to signal and communicate. In Australia, yellow and red flags on the beach indicate swimming conditions. There are no universal standards, but in auto racing a green flag generally means start, yellow means caution, red means stop, and a black and white checked flag means the race is finished. American football uses a yellow flag when a rule is broken, while Canadian football uses an orange flag. Flags are not restricted to the field. Many sports teams have their own flags and fans wave them to show support for their favorite team.

Developing critical thinking

1 Discuss these questions in a group.

1 Which of the emotions in the box on the right do you feel when you see your country's flag? Why?

When I see my country's flag, I feel ... because ...

2 What else can be used on a flag to symbolize a country? Give examples.

Flags can also use ... to symbolize the country, such as ... .

EMOTIONS

brave	happy
calm	interested
confident	proud

2 **Think about the ideas from *Is seeing really believing?* and *Colors and flags* and discuss these questions in a group.**

   1 What do the colors in the box on the right make you think of?

    Black and white reminds me of...
    Dark blue makes me think of...

   2 Did you all agree? Why or why not?

    We did / didn't agree about dark blue.
    It makes me think of..., and it makes my partner think of...

COLORS
black and white
bright yellow
dark blue
light brown
pink

Vocabulary skill

ADDING SUFFIXES TO CHANGE VERBS INTO NOUNS

A suffix is a group of letters added to the end of a word to change its part of speech.

Here are some common suffixes that can change verbs into nouns:

-tion	create → creation	-ance	defy → defiance
-sion	admit → admission	-ence	exist → existence
-ment	commit → commitment		

It is best to consult a dictionary to determine the correct suffix.

1 **Change these verbs into nouns by adding suffixes. You may need to make spelling changes. Then check your answers in a dictionary.**

   1 arrange   _____   **4** inform   _____

   2 appear   _____   **5** depress   _____

   3 depend   _____   **6** restrict   _____

2 **Change these nouns into verbs by removing the suffix. You may need to make spelling changes. Then check your answers in a dictionary.**

   1 composition _____   **4** conclusion _____

   2 management _____   **5** indication _____

   3 preference _____   **6** allowance _____

3 **Make the verbs in the box into nouns by adding the correct suffix. Then complete these sentences with the nouns.**

appoint	assist	compose	confuse	differ	enjoy	replace	suggest

   1 That woman needs help. Can someone please call for _____ ?

   2 My old black ink printer broke. It is time for me to get a _____ .

   3 The old tiles have a beautiful color _____ on them.

   4 I cannot decide what color to paint my room. Do you have a _____ ?

   5 Lisa gets a lot of _____ from helping others.

   6 What is the _____ between an optical and visual illusion?

   7 There seems to be some _____ over the exact name of this color.

   8 I am not well. I need to make an _____ to see a doctor.

WRITING Describing colors

You are going to learn about writing complete sentences, and count and noncount nouns. You are then going to use these to write a paragraph describing what colors symbolize in your culture.

Writing skill

WRITING COMPLETE SENTENCES

A fragment is a piece of a sentence. Fragments cannot stand on their own as a complete sentence. They are common in speaking but should be avoided in writing. Fragments can lack a subject or verb, or begin with words like: *before, after, because, since, unless, until, when, while, if, although.*

<u>Fragments</u>

Has five rings of blue, yellow, black, green, and red. (no subject)

Certain colors of flags in sports. (no verb)

Since they adopted the U.N flag in 1947.

If the U.N. wants to change its flag.

<u>Sentences</u>

The Olympic flag has five rings of blue, yellow, black, green, and red.

Certain colors of flags in sports are used to communicate.

Since they adopted the U.N flag in 1947, it has changed slightly.

It will not be easy if the U.N. wants to change its flag.

1 **Read these items. Write *F* (fragment) or *S* (sentence).**

1 After we got home last night. ____

2 Many flags in the Middle East contain the color green. ____

3 Yemen's flag is three horizontal stripes of red, white, and black. ____

4 Because I study English. ____

5 I cannot tell the difference between violet and purple. ____

6 The colors in the sunset were beautiful. ____

7 The color that I like the most. ____

8 When I wake up every morning. ____

2 **There are four fragments in this paragraph. Rewrite the fragments as sentences.**

The background on the South Korean flag is white. Because white is a traditional color of the Korean people. The blue and red circle in the center. It represents the origins of everything in the universe. The circle represents opposites. Such as positive and negative and night and day. The black lines around the circle represent the elements of fire, water, earth, wood, and metal. After you understand the symbolism behind this or any flag. You appreciate it more.

Grammar

COUNT AND NONCOUNT NOUNS

Count nouns

Count nouns are nouns that we can count. They can be singular (e.g. *flag, color, box*) or plural (e.g. *flags, colors, boxes*).

Noncount nouns

Noncount nouns are nouns that we cannot count. They can only be singular (e.g. *freedom, peace, water*). Study these categories of noncount nouns:

Category	Examples
1 Liquids	coffee, milk, tea, oil, _____
2 Solids	bread, butter, meat, silver, _____
3 Small particles	flour, hair, sand, sugar, _____
4 Collective (group) nouns	furniture, food, luggage, _____
5 Abstract nouns	fun, health, honesty, peace, _____
6 Fields of study	chemistry, law, philosophy, _____
7 Natural phenomena	rain, sunshine, thunder, _____

1 **Complete the grammar box above. Use the nouns in the box below. There are two nouns for each category.**

Arabic	cheese	clothing	engineering	friendship	gasoline
gold	heat	information	money	rice	salt	water	weather

2 **Read these sentences. Write C (count) or N (noncount) for the words in bold.**

1 If you want me to make **cookies** (___), please buy some **flour** (___), and **sugar** (___).
2 The **weather** (___) was terrible on our **vacation** (___). There was **rain** (___) every **day** (___).
3 Our **teacher** (___) said our **homework** (___) is not due until **Tuesday** (___).
4 At my **university** (___) lots of **students** (___) study **economics** (___).
5 Can you buy some **bread** (___), **cheese** (___), **fruit** (___), and **carrots** (___).
6 This brown **furniture** (___) is not **wood** (___). It is some kind of cheap **plastic** (___).

3 Circle **the nouns. Then correct the sentences.**

1 It takes a lot of patiences to teach children.
2 Iris never tells lies. She always tells the truths.
3 I need some advice on finding a job where I can use my Englishes.
4 The informations in these brochures is not accurate.
5 That department store sells both food and furnitures.
6 This meat needs salts and this sauce needs pepper.
7 The color red can represent bloods and courage.
8 The chemicals in the waters make it look orange.

WRITING TASK

Read this paragraph. <u>Underline</u> the count nouns. (Circle) the noncount nouns. There is one sentence fragment. Make it a sentence.

Like many colors, yellow, blue, and green can have different meanings in different cultures. In my culture, yellow often means a lack of bravery. If you are afraid of something, you might be considered "yellow." We also have an expression "yellow journalism." This refers to journalism that is not always 100% true. Yellow is also used to mean slow down. Since it's the middle color on traffic lights. The color blue can represent sadness. For example, the expressions "to feel blue" and "to have the blues" mean to feel very sad. The color green can have several meanings in my culture. It can symbolize spring, growth, and nature. It can represent recycling and environmentalism. It can even represent money because our currency is green. Also, if you say someone is "green" it means that they don't have very much experience. I'm not sure why we say that!

BRAINSTORM

Choose three colors. What do they symbolize in your culture? Do they have more than one meaning? Are there expressions in your language or examples that can help illustrate the meaning? Complete the word map with your ideas.

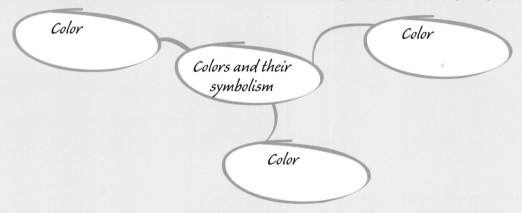

PLAN

Plan a paragraph describing what the three colors symbolize in your culture. Look back at your brainstorm and write a topic sentence. Choose the most interesting information to include in your paragraph.

WRITE

Write your paragraph. Pay attention to your use of count and noncount nouns. Avoid fragments.

SHARE

Exchange paragraphs with a partner. Look at the checklist on page 109 and provide feedback to your partner.

REWRITE AND EDIT

Consider your partner's comments and rewrite your paragraph.

Studying with others

by Stella Cottrell

Most courses schedule groupwork of one kind or another because they value the additional learning which takes place.

Contexts

Some of the contexts in which you may be required to work with others include:

- seminars
- discussion groups
- group projects
- support groups
- mentor schemes
- lab groups
- work placements

The format of these will vary, but there are basic principles and skills common to many different group contexts.

Identify one occasion when you were in a group that worked particularly well.

What made the group successful? How did that group differ from other groups you have taken part in?

Working co-operatively

Working co-operatively creates opportunities to:

- share ideas – so each of you has more ideas
- see extra perspectives and points of view, which otherwise you might not have considered
- benefit from a wider pool of experience, background knowledge, and other styles of work
- stimulate each other's thinking
- clarify your own thinking through talking and through answering questions
- gain others' help in staying focused on the main point – so you can explore a thought with the group
- learn to deal with challenge and criticism
- realize there are more dimensions and answers to a question than you can discover on your own.

Self-evaluation: studying with other people

Rate yourself on the following aspects of studying with others.

Aspect	1 very weak	2 weak	3 ok	4 good	5 excellent
Appreciating what other people have to offer					
Listening to what other people say					
Making a point effectively in groups					
Understanding how to plan for successful groupwork					
Knowing how to be an effective group member					
Knowing how to deal with difficulties in a group					
Understanding how to deal with unfairness in groups					
Contributing effectively to seminars					
Knowing how to share study without cheating					
Making an effective oral presentation					

Extremes

READING	Finding similarities and differences Identifying the source
VOCABULARY	Understanding compound words
WRITING	Using transitions to add and emphasize information
GRAMMAR	Expressing ability

Discussion point

Take this quiz. Then discuss with a partner.

1 How high is Mount Everest, the world's highest mountain?
  a 6,848 meters **b** 8,848 meters **c** 10,848 meters
2 The Mariana Trench is the lowest point on Earth. Where is it?
  a the Atlantic Ocean **b** the Pacific Ocean **c** the Indian Ocean
3 At over 10,000 meters, the highest mountain measured from the ocean floor to the peak is called Mauna Kea. Which U.S. state is it in?
  a Hawaii **b** California **c** Alaska

I think the answer to question ... is ... . What do you think?

Vocabulary preview

Complete these sentences. Use the words in the box.

concerned	convince	dedicated	eventually	expedition
firsthand	investigate	operate	species	

1 Dan experienced a sunrise _____ on Mt. Kilimanjaro.
2 My advisor tried to _____ me to study marine biology.
3 Several fish _____ were in danger after the oil spill.
4 I believe _____ scientists will solve climate change.
5 Are you _____ about the threat of rising sea levels?
6 The submarine was designed to _____ under the Arctic ice.
7 Jean is _____ to educating people about the ocean.
8 Scientists plan to _____ the stones found under the sea.
9 The team is preparing to lead an _____ to the South Pole.

READING 1 Earth's final frontier

Before you read

Why do people study the oceans? Do you think it is important to study the oceans? Why or why not? Discuss with a partner.

I believe people study the oceans because ...
I do / don't think it's important to study the oceans because ...

Global reading

Scan *Earth's final frontier*. Complete these sentences with numbers.

1 *Alvin's* first dive was to _____ meters.
2 *Shinkai 6500* weighs _____ tons.
3 *Jiaolong's* first dive was in the year _____.
4 *Jiaolong* is designed to dive to _____ meters.
5 The deepest point in the ocean is _____ meters.

Close reading

FINDING SIMILARITIES AND DIFFERENCES

Items, concepts, and ideas can be compared and contrasted in a text. Comparing focuses on similarities and contrasting focuses on differences. Recognizing when comparisons and contrasts are being made will help you to understand the text's main ideas.

Words that signal ...

- similarities: *like, also, as well, both, neither*
- differences: *unlike, but, however, while, whereas*

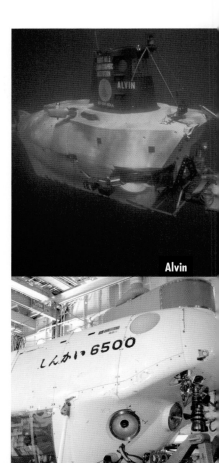

Alvin

Shinkai 6500

1 **Read *Earth's final frontier*. Highlight the words that indicate similarities in one color. Highlight the words that indicate differences in another color.**

2 Complete the Venn diagram about similarities and differences between *Alvin* and *Shinkai 6500*. Use the words in the box. Then find three more ideas in *Earth's final frontier* and add these to the diagram.

can dive for nine hours   can dive to 6,500 meters   holds two pilots and a researcher   is 7 meters long   is 9.5 meters long   maps the ocean floor   operates in global waters   researches underwater earthquakes

Alvin / Shinkai 6500

named after a researcher — *investigates new species*

ACADEMIC KEYWORDS

discovery	(n)	/dɪˈskʌvəri/
record	(v)	/rɪˈkɔrd/
version	(n)	/ˈvɜrʒ(ə)n/

EARTH'S FINAL FRONTIER

[1] Have you ever wondered what lies deep below the ocean's surface? If so, you are not alone. Over the past few decades, engineers have developed submersible technologies to explore these extreme ocean depths. Submersibles are smaller versions of submarines. They can go much deeper than submarines but require a mother ship at the surface. Two of the most remarkable are the United States' *Alvin* and Japan's *Shinkai 6500*.

[2] *Alvin*, the first deep-sea submersible, was named after the dedicated researcher Allyn Vine. It made its first dive in 1964 and still makes hundreds of expeditions a year. It is constantly being rebuilt with the latest technologies. It operates in global waters and has made some amazing discoveries, including over 300 new species. In 1986, it made 12 dives to the *Titanic* to photograph the famous shipwreck firsthand. Alvin's first dive in 1964 was to 11 meters, but these days it is able to dive to 4,500 meters.

[3] *Shinkai 6500*, which means "deep sea" in Japanese, made its first dive in 1990. As its name suggests, *Shinkai 6500* can dive to 6,500 meters. Like *Alvin*, it also operates in global waters, investigates new species, researches underwater earthquakes and volcanoes, and maps the ocean floor.

[4] Weather patterns are recorded in the type of sediment in the seafloor. *Shinkai 6500* can collect samples of this sediment for analysis. Hopefully, this will help researchers better understand the causes of climate change. Scientists have a good idea about how the ocean's surface is warming. However, they are concerned because they know little about how the deep ocean is warming.

[5] Neither submersible is very big. *Alvin* is seven meters long and weighs 17 tons, while *Shinkai 6500* is 9.5 meters and weighs 26.7 tons. *Alvin* can dive for nine hours but *Shinkai 6500* can only dive for eight. However, it dives at a deeper depth. Both can hold three people. *Shinkai 6500* can hold two pilots and one researcher, whereas *Alvin* can hold one pilot and two researchers. Both have three windows and two robot arms. These arms are able to bring up material from the ocean depths for further study.

[6] One of the newest submersibles is China's *Jiaolong*. During its first dive in 2010, it was able to reach a depth of over 3,500 meters. In 2011, it was able to reach 5,000 meters. *Jiaolong* is designed to reach depths of 7,000 meters. Incredibly, this would allow *Jiaolong* to reach 99.8% of the ocean floor. Eventually, submersibles will be able to reach 100%.

DID YOU KNOW… the deepest point is **11,033 meters**, in the Pacific Ocean?

Developing critical thinking

Discuss these questions in a group.

1 Is exploring the ocean floor a good way of spending time and money?

Exploring the ocean floor is / isn't a good way to spend money because …

2 Which of the dangers in the box on the right are underwater explorers most likely to face? Why?

I think underwater explorers are most likely to face … because …

3 Would you ever go down in a submersible? Why or why not?

I would / wouldn't go down in a submersible because …

DANGERS

animal attacks
cold temperature
darkness
getting lost
poor weather
problems with equipment

READING 2 Super Sherpa

Before you read

Look at the picture. What do you see? Where do you think the picture was taken? Why do you think the trash is there? Discuss with a partner.

In the picture I see ... I think the picture was taken ... Perhaps the trash is there because ...

Global reading

■ IDENTIFYING THE SOURCE ▐

Texts can come from a variety of sources, each with its own writing style. Identifying the source gives you important information about the writer and his or her message. Possible sources include …

- scientific journals: texts have academic vocabulary and long sentences
- newspapers: texts have simpler language
- opinion columns and blogs: texts have an informal writing style

The layout of a text can also help you quickly identify the source.

Skim *Super Sherpa*. Check (✓) the source.

1 ☐ Scientific journal on climate change
2 ☐ Newspaper article in travel section
3 ☐ Environmental newsmagazine

Close reading

1 Read *Super Sherpa*. Write *M* (main idea) or *S* (supporting detail).

Paragraph 1: He campaigns against climate change and helps to improve the lives of many people in his native Nepal. ___

Paragraph 2: Apa is from a village in Nepal called Thame, which is also the hometown of another famous Sherpa—Tenzing Norgay. ___

Paragraph 3: Apa never planned on becoming a famous mountain climber. ___

Paragraph 4: That year the team displayed a sign that said "Stop Climate Change" at the top of Everest. ___

Paragraph 5: As Apa became more well-known for his environmental work, he started to turn more attention to the people of his native Nepal. ___

Paragraph 6: Melting ice clearly makes climbing more dangerous. ___

Paragraph 7: Above all, he wants to convince everyone to change the way we treat the Earth. ___

2 Write the answers to these questions.

1 What are Sherpas known for?
2 What year did Apa climb Mount Everest for the first time?
3 What did the Eco Everest Exhibition sign say?
4 What did Apa found in 2009?
5 Why is Apa known as the "Super Sherpa"?

3 Check (✓) the statements you can infer from *Super Sherpa*.

1 ☐ Apa and Tenzing Norgay were classmates in school.

2 ☐ When he was a boy, Apa's family was not wealthy.

3 ☐ Some people who climb Mount Everest are irresponsible.

4 ☐ In 2009 Apa climbed Mount Everest alone.

5 ☐ Apa cares about the people and environment of Nepal.

6 ☐ Apa no longer climbs mountains.

[1] Apa may be a small shy man but he has been to the top of the world more times than anyone else. In fact, he has climbed Mount Everest more than twenty times. He campaigns against climate change and helps to improve the lives of many people in his native Nepal.

[2] Apa is a Sherpa. Sherpas are known for their ability to carry heavy loads for long distances at high altitudes. Apa is from a village in Nepal called Thame, which is also the hometown of another famous Sherpa—Tenzing Norgay. In 1953, Tenzing and Edmund Hillary were the first two people to climb to the top of Mount Everest.

[3] Apa never planned on becoming a famous mountain climber. When he was about 12 years old, his father died. He had to quit school and find work to help his family. He started to carry loads uphill for mountain climbing groups in the Himalayas. Later, he worked as a cook and, eventually, he began carrying loads on Everest itself. He worked like this for many years. In 1990, he climbed to the top of Mount Everest for the first time. By 1993, he had stood on top of the world five times in three years.

[4] Over the years, Apa watched dozens of expeditions leave behind old tents, oxygen tanks, ropes, and other equipment. He became increasingly concerned about the environmental impact of these expeditions and climate change. In 2009, he was a member of The Eco Everest Expedition whose purpose was to investigate and raise awareness about climate change. That year the team displayed a sign that said "Stop Climate Change" at the top of Everest. They also removed over 5,000 kilograms of trash from Everest.

[5] As Apa became more well-known for his environmental work, he started to turn more attention to the people of his native Nepal. He used some of his earnings to open a primary school to provide better education for the children of his country. In 2009, he founded the Apa Sherpa Foundation. The foundation is dedicated to improving the education and economic development of the Nepalese people.

[6] These days, Apa spends much of his time traveling and speaking on the subject of climate change. He emphasizes that in the short period of time he has been climbing Everest, he has seen climate change firsthand. When he first started climbing Everest, there was snow and ice on all of the trails, but now there is exposed rock. Melting ice clearly makes climbing more dangerous. Indeed, it is very clear to Apa that climate change is affecting his part of the world.

[7] Apa has been called the "Super Sherpa" for the ease with which he climbs mountains. However, Apa once said, "Everest is never easy. Every time it is hard." Climbing Everest may be challenging, but he is facing an even bigger challenge. Above all, he wants to convince everyone to change the way we treat the Earth.

SUPER SHERPA

ACADEMIC KEYWORDS		
awareness	(n)	/əˈwernəs/
increasingly	(adv)	/ɪnˈkrisɪŋli/
period	(n)	/ˈpɪriəd/

Developing critical thinking

1 Discuss these questions in a group.

1 Which of the characteristics in the box on the right would you use to describe Apa Sherpa?

I would describe Apa Sherpa as …

2 How else could Apa Shepra get his message to a wider audience?

Apa Sherpa could get his message out using …

CHARACTERISTICS	
ambitious	mysterious
caring	selfish
humble	strong

2 Think about the ideas from *Earth's final frontier* and *Super Sherpa* and discuss these questions in a group.

   1 What drives people to explore such extreme parts of our Earth?

     I think people explore extreme parts of our Earth because ...

   2 How similar are the researchers in submersibles to people like Apa? Think about the things in the box on the right.

     Both the researchers and Apa are ...
     Apa thinks ... , whereas the researchers think ...

THINK ABOUT:	
background	personality
education	sense of adventure
interests	values

Vocabulary skill

UNDERSTANDING COMPOUND WORDS

Compound words are two or more words that are put together to create a new meaning. They are formed from different parts of speech: noun + noun, adjective + adjective, or adjective + noun. They can be open or closed. Look at the individual words to help you understand the meaning.

Closed	Open
sunset, snowflake	*marine biologist, bus stop*

It can be difficult to determine if a compound word is closed or open. It is best to consult a dictionary.

1 These words are the first part of compound words in the reading texts. Find them and write the compound words.

From *Earth's final frontier*

   1 mother _____

   2 ship _____

   3 earth _____

   4 ocean _____

From *Super Sherpa*

   5 home _____

   6 primary _____

   7 up _____

   8 mountain _____

From both readings

   9 first _____

  10 climate _____

2 Circle the words that make compound words with the words in bold. Then write the compound words. Check your answers in a dictionary.

   1 **base**   ball   side   basket   _____

   2 **stop**   water   go   sign   _____

   3 **work**   easy   high   out   _____

   4 **break**   drink   over   fast   _____

   5 **over**   time   wait   down   _____

3 Write words to make compound words. Check your answers in a dictionary.

   1 air _____   **3** under _____

   2 book _____   **4** head _____

WRITING Giving your opinion

You are going to learn about using transitions to add and emphasize information, and using modals and *be able to* to express ability. You are then going to use these to write a paragraph giving your opinion.

Writing skill

USING TRANSITIONS TO ADD AND EMPHASIZE INFORMATION

Transition words link words, sentences, or paragraphs. Using them correctly helps your writing flow more smoothly and helps the reader follow the writing. Two common types of transitions are for adding and emphasizing information.

Transitions for adding information: *and, also, as well, moreover, in addition*

It operates in global waters **and** has made some amazing discoveries.

Like Alvin, Shinkai 6500 **also** operates in global waters.

Alvin can hold three people. Shinkai can hold three people **as well**.

Deep sea exploration is expensive. **In addition / Moreover**, it can be dangerous.

Transitions for emphasizing information: *clearly, certainly, in fact, above all*

Melting ice **clearly / certainly** makes climbing more dangerous.

In fact, Apa has climbed Mount Everest over 20 times.

Above all, he wants to convince us to change the way we are treating the Earth.

1 **Unscramble the second sentences.**

1 Many of the three million shipwrecks around the world are in the Atlantic Ocean.
   many / in the Caribbean Sea / there / as well / are

2 The main difference between a sea and an ocean is that a sea is smaller.
   is surrounded / a sea / by land / moreover

3 The Pacific Ocean has the largest area of water.
   the largest / by volume / in addition / is / it

4 The warmest sea is the Persian Gulf, at 35 degrees Celsius.
   the most shallow / is / also / it / one of

5 The largest fish in the sea is the whale shark.
   mammal / blue whale / the / and / the largest / heaviest / is

2 **Complete these sentences. Use the words in the box.**

| above all   certainly   clearly   in fact |

1 The Himalayas are _____ some of the most dangerous mountains to climb.

2 Jason wants to climb Mount Everest using a local guide and leaving nothing behind. _____, he wants to do it without the need for oxygen tanks.

3 Climbing the highest mountains on each continent _____ requires a lot of time and money.

4 The Sherpas are experts at mountain terrain. _____, the Sherpas were invaluable to early explorers of the Himalayan Mountains.

Grammar

EXPRESSING ABILITY

We can express ability using *can / could* and *be able to*. Study the forms:

Form	Example
Present ability	
subject + *can* + base form	Submersibles can go deeper than submarines.
subject + *cannot* + base form	Submarines cannot go deeper than submersibles.
subject + *am / is / are* + able to + base form	Submarines are able to go deeper than submarines.
subject + *am not / is not / are not* + able to + base form	Submarines are not able to go deeper than submersibles.
Past ability	
subject + *could* + base form	Researchers could film *Titanic*.
subject + *could not* + base form	Researchers could not leave *Alvin*.
subject + *was / were* + able to + base form	Researchers were able to film *Titanic*.
subject + *was not / were not* + able to + base form	Researchers were not able to leave *Alvin*.

Use *be able to* (not *could*) in affirmative sentences for single actions.
During Jialong's first dive, it was able to reach a depth of 3,500 meters.

1 **Complete this message. Circle the correct words in bold.**

> Hi Jon,
>
> I'm sorry but I (1) **cannot / am able to** drive you to the airport. I
> (2) **cannot / could not** get my car started this morning, and I
> (3) **could not / am not able to** take it to the garage now because
> it's closed. I (4) **could / am able to** start it yesterday so I'm not sure
> what's wrong with it. Maybe Mark (5) **can / was able to** drive you? I
> (6) **cannot / could not** find his number now but will see him later. I'll
> ask him to call you.
>
> Talk soon,
>
> Craig

2 **Rewrite these sentences. Express ability in a different way.**

1 I am not able to swim.
2 Ben could not make it to the top of the mountain.
3 Kamal can name over a hundred types of tropical fish.
4 My brother and I could go camping by ourselves as kids.
5 Richard was not able to win his first swimming race last month.

WRITING TASK

Read this paragraph. <u>Underline</u> the ways to express ability. (Circle) the transitions that add or emphasize information.

Team sports such as baseball and volleyball can teach us a lot about life. First, sports can show us that we need to work hard. For example, we may need to pace ourselves and have endurance to achieve our aims. In addition, practice is important if we want to be good at a sport. I couldn't play basketball well in high school but I kept practicing and now I can play well. Second, sports clearly prepare students for the real world. Players learn how to work together and get along. They learn how to solve problems as well. In fact, all of these are essential skills for working in any business or organization. Third, sports also teach us about failing. Winning isn't everything. Every game or sport will have a winner and a loser, and sports are able to teach us that it's OK to lose sometimes, if you try your best. Moreover, we often learn more from our failures than our successes.

BRAINSTORM

Read the opinions about sports in the box. Choose one you agree with and complete the table. Write three reasons that support your opinion.

> Extreme sports can be dangerous and should be banned.
> High school students should not be required to play sports.
> People spend too much time watching sports on TV.
> Professional athletes can make excellent role models.
> Sports are able to bring enemies together.

Opinion	
Reason 1	
Reason 2	
Reason 3	

PLAN

Plan a paragraph giving your opinion. Look back at your brainstorm and write a topic sentence. Support your opinion with reasons.

WRITE

Write your paragraph. Use transition words to add or emphasize information. Pay attention to how you express ability.

SHARE

Exchange paragraphs with a partner. Look at the checklist on page 109 and provide feedback to your partner.

REWRITE AND EDIT

Consider your partner's comments and rewrite your paragraph. Check any compound words in a dictionary.

STUDY SKILLS Using computers for effective study

Getting started

Discuss these questions with a partner.

1 What do you use computers for?
2 Do you enjoy using a computer? Why or why not?
3 What are some benefits of using a computer to write your assignments?

Scenario

Read this scenario. Think about what Ingrid is doing right and what she is doing wrong. What would be the advantages to Ingrid of using a computer instead?

Consider it

Read these seven tips for using a computer for studying. Discuss each one with a partner. What other tips can you name?

1 **Formatting** Learn how to format your work, and how to create charts, tables, and graphs. A typed document with an attractive font, neat margins, and page numbers can make a better impression than a handwritten one.

2 **Editing** A computer allows you to revise your work easily. Add, rearrange, remove, or replace information. Do not rewrite the whole text for each draft.

3 **Word count** Learn to use the word count function to save time.

4 **Grammar and spelling** The grammar and spell check functions are helpful, but should not be relied on entirely.

5 **Dictionary and thesaurus** Use the dictionary and thesaurus functions to help you be more precise in what you are trying to communicate.

6 **Researching** Use the Internet for research purposes. The Internet can also help with fact checking.

7 **Saving your work** Back up your work regularly. When you finish, save your work for future reference.

Over to you

Discuss these questions with a partner.

1 What is something related to computers that you would like to learn more about?
2 Can you name any drawbacks to using a computer for studying?
3 Do you think computer literacy is important? Why or why not?

When Ingrid has a writing assignment, she always writes her first draft on a piece of paper. She then revises her draft on a different piece of paper. She often adds, rearranges, removes, or replaces text as she rewrites. After that she edits her work. She uses her dictionary to check her spelling and then checks to make sure her grammar is OK. She sometimes notices and corrects sentence fragments. When she is ready to create her final draft, she writes it carefully and neatly on a piece of paper and gives it to her teacher. Ingrid's teacher has said her students are free to write their assignments like Ingrid does, or use a computer.

READING	Summarizing
	Identifying reasons
VOCABULARY	Finding the correct
	definition of a word
WRITING	Using transitions to
	sequence events
GRAMMAR	The simple past
	tense

Discussion point

Discuss these questions with a partner.

1 What do you feel are the most important things in life?

   I feel the most important things in life are ...

2 What do you want to achieve in your life?

   In my life, I want to achieve ...

3 Read these stages in life. Which do you think is the best to be in? Why?

   I think the best stage in life is ... because ...

infancy (birth–18 months)

early childhood (18 months–5 years)

middle childhood (6–8 years)

pre-teen years (9–12 years)

teen years (13–18 years)

early adulthood (19–30 years)

middle adulthood (31–55 years)

late adulthood (56+ years)

Vocabulary preview

Complete these sentences. Use the words in the box.

adolescent	capability	discard	familiar
resistant	sustain	technical	transition

1 At what age does an _____ become an adult?

2 I am not _____ with that folktale. Can you explain it?

3 _____ old cell phones and other electronics safely.

4 The _____ help that the engineer provided was very useful.

5 This machine has the _____ to be ten times faster than humans.

6 My father is _____ to my idea of studying abroad next year.

7 The _____ from middle school to high school is hard.

8 Rod could not _____ his expensive lifestyle after he lost his job.

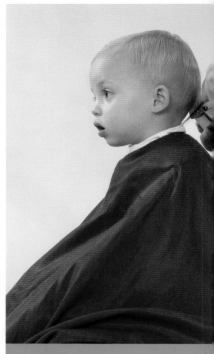

RITES OF PASSAGE

first birthday	first job
first haircut	marriage
21ˢᵗ birthday	first child
graduation	retirement

READING 1 Coming of age

Before you read

1 **Which of the rites of passage in the box on the right are important in your culture? Which are not? Discuss with a partner.**

... is/isn't important in my culture.

2 **Look at page 89. Predict what age group the text will be about.**

Global reading

Skim *Coming of age*. Check your prediction.

Close reading

> **SUMMARIZING**
>
> When we summarize a text, we reduce it to its key points. Writing a summary helps you determine essential ideas and understand important details. Highlighting and annotating (unit 3) and taking notes (unit 5) all make summarizing easier. Study these tips for writing effective summaries:
>
> • Identify the main ideas and key details. Ignore irrelevant information.
>
> • Use your own words. Do not copy or just change a couple of words.
>
> • Try to keep the same order as the original information.
>
> • Write only enough to convey the gist (main meaning) of the text.

Highlight and annotate *Coming of age*, or take notes. Then complete the summary.

The formal transition to becoming an (1) _____ exists in every culture. The coming-of-age rite of (2) _____ can start with a separation from what is usual. There is then some instruction or (3) _____ by an older person, followed by a stage where the young person is (4) _____ as an adult. For example, in Brazil people become adults when they get a (5) _____. In Japan, there is an official (6) _____ for 20-year-olds. In Vanuatu, men show their manhood by land (7) _____. There are different ways of celebrating an adolescent's coming of age, but they all represent the recognition of becoming an adult and what that (8) _____ means.

Coming of AGE

[1] The formal passage from childhood into adulthood is universal, with all cultures having traditions, rites, and ceremonies that recognize this familiar transition. This rite of passage is known as "coming of age." In general, cultures share similarities in this passage. For many, there is some sort of separation from normality, followed by instruction or preparation from an elder. A transitional stage, which sometimes includes a test, is then followed by the person being recognized as an adult. Let's take a look at three such passages around the world.

[2] In Brazil, getting a driver's license is a major step toward becoming an adult. It provides a sense of freedom and individuality. The legal age to obtain a license is 18. People need to take classes and pass technical and practical tests before they get a license. Driving in Brazil, like in any country, can be dangerous. The younger people who take the required courses have proven to be very good drivers and sustain lower accident rates than older drivers.

[3] Coming of Age Day is a national holiday in Japan. It takes place the second Monday in January. All young adults who turned or will turn 20 years old between April 1 of the previous year and March 31 of the current year can attend an official ceremony held at local government offices. Men and women dress up in traditional clothes, which include kimono for the women. Officials give speeches and present small gifts. After the ceremony, the "new" adults get together with friends to celebrate. They now have the capability to go out into society as adults with the responsibilities and knowledge they have acquired.

[4] In the South Pacific nation of Vanuatu, young boys and adolescent men participate in a daring land-diving ceremony. They climb up a 25-meter wooden tower. Once they have tied vines to their feet, they dive off headfirst. It is believed that when the land diver touches the earth with his head, it will bring a good harvest for the year. A diver's mother may hold a diver's favorite possession from his childhood during the jump. When the young man completes his first dive, this item is then discarded as a symbol of him reaching manhood. Any mistake in measuring the vine length or tower height can result in serious injury.

[5] Coming-of-age ceremonies and other rites of passage are ways of marking the passing of time. Children become adolescents and adolescents become adults. Cultures develop ways of putting meaning to these transitions. We have all come through such passages. You might be resistant to the idea of jumping off a wooden tower with vines tied to your feet, but you have certainly listened to the people who have come before you and taken some of their advice. You have the responsibility to pass on your knowledge to those who follow you.

ACADEMIC KEYWORDS		
formal	(adj)	/ˈfɔrm(ə)l/
obtain	(v)	/əbˈteɪn/
traditional	(adj)	/trəˈdɪʃən(ə)l/

The "new" adults get together with friends to celebrate.

"It is believed that when the land diver touches the earth with his head, it will bring a good harvest for the year."

Developing critical thinking

Discuss these questions in a group.

1 When are people considered an adult in your culture?

I think people are considered an adult in my culture when they are ...

2 When did you feel you were no longer a child? Why?

I felt I was no longer a child when I was ... years old, because ...

3 When do you think people should do the things in the box on the right? Why?

I think people should ... when they are about ... years old, because ...

LIFE EVENTS	
buy a home	go to college
get a job	have children
get married	

READING 2 Gardening 380 kilometers above Earth

Before you read

Some astronauts grow plants in space. Why do you think they do this? How do you think plants in space might differ from plants on Earth? What could be some of the challenges of growing plants in space? Discuss with a partner.

I think astronauts grow plants in space because ...
Plants in space might be more ... or less ... than plants on Earth.
The challenges of growing plants in space could be ...

Global reading

Skim *Gardening 380 kilometers above Earth*. Check (✓) the best sub-title.

1 ☐ How to make the moon green
2 ☐ Why space plants taste better
3 ☐ Growing plants in space

Close reading

1 **Highlight and annotate *Gardening 380 kilometers above Earth*, or take notes. Then write a summary.**

> **■ IDENTIFYING REASONS ■**
>
> A text may contain one or more reasons why a particular event or action occurs. Identifying *why* things happen helps you to understand the text.
>
> Words that signal reasons: *because, due to, since, as*

2 **Write the answers to these questions.**
   1 Why did early explorers take seeds and plants with them?
   2 Why is it impractical to take all the food needed for long space journeys?
   3 Why can plants help improve air quality on long space journeys?
   4 Why does the oxygen that plants produce in space stay around the plants?
   5 Why are special gels used to sustain plant growth in space?

3 **Read these sentences from *Gardening 380 kilometers above Earth*. Write the words the pronouns in bold refer to.**
   1 Since early explorers wanted familiar foods to ease their transition to foreign lands, **they** often took seeds and plants with **them**.

   a they = _____   b them = _____

   2 Due to the lack of gravity in space, the oxygen that the plants produce stays around the plants. **This** can actually kill **them**.

   a this = _____   b them = _____

   3 As soil is too heavy to send to space, special gels are used to sustain plant growth. **These** retain water and deliver **it** to the plants.

   a these= _____   b it = _____

GARDENING
380
KILOMETERS
ABOVE
EARTH

[1] Astronauts go through physical, psychological, and technical training, but there is one kind of training many people do not know about. Astronauts also go through training in how to care for plants. These "astronaut gardeners" are growing vegetables and other plants in space. Humans aren't the only life forms on the International Space Station. They share their work and living space with plants.

[2] Taking plants along on a trip isn't a new idea. Since early explorers wanted familiar foods to ease their transition to foreign lands, they often took seeds and plants with them. Space travelers do much the same thing. In fact, as space trips become longer it will be necessary to grow food in space. A nine-month trip to Mars, each way, would require huge amounts of food and water. The cost of taking anything into space is about $22,000 per kilogram. Because of this, it's not practical to send everything needed for such a long journey, only to be used once and discarded. Everything used in space must have several uses.

[3] This is why growing plants in space will be so important. Plants can serve many uses on a long space journey. They are a renewable food source. Astronauts will welcome the addition of fresh fruits and vegetables to their diet of dry foods. Also, because plants use carbon dioxide and produce oxygen, they can help improve air quality. Currently all oxygen is taken aboard in tanks and then caught again so it can be reused. Plants can help extend the capabilities of the air inside the spacecraft—the only air that the astronauts can breathe.

[4] However, there are challenges with growing plants in space. Due to the lack of gravity in space, the oxygen that the plants produce stays around the plants. This can actually kill them, so fans are needed to circulate the air. Without gravity, roots don't "know" to grow down, leaves don't know to grow up, and water doesn't easily travel up the roots to the leaves. Specialized containers are being developed to help the plants grow correctly. There are challenges with soil as well. As soil is too heavy to send to space, special liquid gels are used to sustain plant growth. These retain water and deliver it to the plants.

[5] Scientists are also working on the plants themselves. They are trying to breed plants to grow more efficiently and to grow with less water and light. They are also looking for ways to make plants more resistant to disease. Moreover, such innovations in plant breeding could result in improvements back here on Earth. Imagine growing plants in places where light, water, and weather are less than ideal. Deserts may one day provide lots of fresh food for local people, saving transportation costs. Similarly, many diseases now harm or kill plants. Plants that are resistant to disease could provide an important new food source. With the world's population now at seven billion people, our astronaut gardeners may help discover ways to feed those billions.

Astronauts also go through training in how to care for plants.

ACADEMIC KEYWORDS

necessary	(adj)	/ˈnesəˌseri/
quality	(n)	/ˈkwɑləti/
result	(v)	/rɪˈzʌlt/

Developing critical thinking

1 Discuss these questions in a group.

1 Which of the personality traits in the box on the right would someone need to be an astronaut? Why?

I think an astronaut would need to be very ... because ...

2 What kinds of things do you think astronauts miss most?

Astronauts probably miss ... most because ...

PERSONALITY TRAITS

adaptable	flexible
decisive	independent
determined	patient

2 **Think about the ideas from *Coming of age* and *Gardening 380 kilometers above Earth* and discuss these questions in a group.**

1 What achievements do you hope the next generation accomplishes? Think about the areas in the box on the right.

   I hope the next generation accomplishes ... because ...

2 Do you think it is likely the next generation will accomplish the things you discussed in question 1? Why or why not?

   I think it's likely / unlikely that the next generation will accomplish ... because ...

THINK ABOUT:

education   health
environment   space travel
food   technology

Vocabulary skill

FINDING THE CORRECT DEFINITION OF A WORD

When you look up a word in a dictionary, there is usually more than one definition. It is necessary to find the definition you need. First, determine what part of speech the word is. Then look at the other words in the sentence to help you choose the right definition. Note which definition number goes with each sentence below.

1 Astronauts are looking for ways to make plants more resistant to disease.

2 At first he was resistant to the idea of his son becoming an astronaut.

resistant /rɪˈzɪst(ə)nt/ (adj)

1 not harmed or affected by something

2 opposed to something

1 **Read the dictionary entry for the word *source* on the right. Write the numbers of the definitions next to these sentences.**

   a His son was a constant **source** of worry to him. ____

   b For centuries, the **source** of the Nile was a mystery. ____

   c His garden was the **source** for all this fresh food. ____

2 **Read the dictionary entry for the word *respect* on the right. Write the numbers of the definitions next to these sentences.**

   a The coming-of-age ceremony gave him **respect** for his culture. ____

   b Coming-of-age ceremonies differ in some **respects**. ____

   c Doctors need to **respect** the wishes of their patients. ____

   d It is important to show your **respect** to your elders. ____

   e I **respect** people who put others before themselves. ____

source /sɔrs/

NOUN [C]

1 a person, place, or thing that provides something that you need or want

2 the cause of a problem, or the place where it began

3 the beginning of a river or stream

respect /rɪˈspekt/

NOUN [U]

1 the attitude that someone is important and should be admired, and that you should treat them politely

2 **respect for sth** a feeling that something is important and deserves serious attention

3 an aspect of something

respect /rɪˈspekt/

VERB [T]

4 to treat someone in a way that shows that you think they are important and should be admired

5 to understand the importance of something

WRITING Describing a memorable day

You are going to learn about using transitions to sequence events, and using the simple past tense. You are then going to use these to describe a memorable day.

Writing skill

▮ **USING TRANSITIONS TO SEQUENCE EVENTS** ▮▮▮▮▮

In addition to adding and emphasizing information (unit 8), transitions can be used to show whether two events happened at different times or at the same time. This helps the reader follow a series of events. Ideas and events are often, but not always, presented in the order they occur.

Transitions for showing …

- two events happened at different times: *first, before, then, later, once, second, after, afterward, when, as soon as*

  *People take formal classes **before** they can receive a driver's license.*

  ***After** the ceremony the "new" adults get together with their friends.*

- two events happened at the same time: *during, while, meanwhile, in the meantime, at the same time*

  *Astronauts grow food. **At the same time** they take some food with them.*

  *People show off their traditional clothes **while** officials give speeches.*

1 **Read these sentences about coming of age. Circle the correct transition words in bold.**

1 "I'm currently doing volunteer work overseas and I feel like the experience is changing me. I don't know what I'll do **after / while** I go home. **During / Meanwhile**, back home, my parents would like me to come back soon and get a job, but I'm not sure I'm ready. I can do that **later / at the same time**." Emiko, 22, Japan

2 "**When / During** I was 14 I got my first cell phone. **Before / In the meantime** that my parents wouldn't allow it, so that was a big deal for me! I was able to talk to my friends and family anytime and, **first / at the same time**, I suddenly felt very grown up." Leila, 17, Egypt

3 "I'll never forget my 16th birthday. There were two things I did that day. **First / While**, I got my driver's license. I did that in the morning. **When / Second**, I bought an old car. My parents gave me the money. **After that / Before** I wasn't able to drive anywhere." Rory, 20, U.S.A.

4 "I felt like an adult **once / first** I moved out of my parents' home. **While / Then** I was in school my parents treated me like a typical teenager. But **before / as soon as** I got my own place I felt more independent." Alberto, 25, Brazil

2 **Complete these sentences with your own ideas.**

1 After I get home tonight, I want to _____.

2 Before I go to bed I like to _____.

3 I do not like to _____ during class.

4 Once I finish this class I plan to _____.

5 I am doing this exercise. Meanwhile, the teacher is _____.

6 As soon as I finish this exercise, I hope to _____.

Grammar

THE SIMPLE PAST TENSE

Use the simple past tense in these situations ...

1 A specific, completed past action: *I cleaned my room last night.*
2 A series of completed past actions: *I went home. Then I had dinner.*
3 Past actions over a period of time: *I lived in Spain for a year.*
4 Habits or repeated past actions: *I usually went to class.*

Study the forms:

Form	Example
Regular verbs not ending in -e, -y, or vowel + consonant verb + -ed	work → worked
Verbs ending in -e verb + -d	taste → tasted
Verbs ending in -y (verb -y) + -ied (verb -y) + -ed	try → tried play → played
Verbs ending in vowel + consonant verb + double consonant + -ed	jog → jogged
You must memorize irregular verbs	take → took, go → went
Negative did not + base form	did not work

1 **Complete these sentences. Use the simple past form of the verbs in parentheses.**

1 I _____ (get) married three years ago. We just _____ (have) our first child.

2 I _____ (not go) to my graduation ceremony. I _____ (break) my leg two days before so I was in the hospital.

3 I _____ (buy) my first laptop last month. Before that I _____ (share) one with my sister.

4 My father _____ (retire) last year. He _____ (work) for the same company for 45 years.

5 My mother _____ (tell) me that I _____ (not lose) my first tooth until I _____ (turn) seven.

2 **Complete this paragraph. Use the simple past tense of the verbs in the box.**

feel	get	hold	not find	scream	stand	study	take

I (1) _____ really nervous when I (2) _____ my driver's license test. I (3) _____ in line for 15 minutes before I finally (4) _____ my test paper. I (5) _____ the test very difficult because I (6) _____ a lot for it. As soon as I (7) _____ my driver's license in my hand I (8) _____! I was really happy that day.

WRITING TASK

Read this paragraph. <u>Underline</u> the verbs in the simple past tense. (Circle) the transition words that indicate sequence.

I remember my high school graduation very well. Besides my immediate family, a lot of my aunts, uncles, and cousins came to the ceremony. I put on my graduation gown and cap and we all drove to the ceremony. It didn't last very long. Some people gave speeches and then they presented awards. We all just sat there quietly during all that. Next, they handed us our diplomas. While we stood in line to receive them, my mother took a lot of photos and my brother tried to make me laugh. I think my mom cried a little. Once I got my diploma, I felt really fantastic. After everyone had their diplomas, we all threw our graduation caps up in the air. That's a fun tradition. Later, at home, my friends and family gave me cards and presents. I had a great day.

BRAINSTORM

Read the occasions in the box. Choose one and complete the table about a memorable day you have had. Write the main events of the day in order.

> a memorable celebration   a time I got good news   a time I won something
> a trip to remember   my first day of school   the day I graduated

Occasion
First
Next
Next
Next
Next
Last

PLAN

Plan a paragraph describing your memorable day. Look back at your brainstorm and write a topic sentence. Think about additional details you could add.

WRITE

Write your paragraph. Pay attention to your use of the simple past tense. Use a variety of transitions to sequence your paragraph.

SHARE

Exchange paragraphs with a partner. Look at the checklist on page 109 and provide feedback to your partner. Use a dictionary to look up any words you do not know.

REWRITE AND EDIT

Consider your partner's comments and rewrite your paragraph.

STUDY SKILLS Making the most of your dictionary

Getting started

Discuss these questions with a partner.

1 How many dictionaries do you own?
2 What kinds of dictionaries have you used?
3 What is the main thing you use a dictionary for? How often do you use one?

Scenario

Read this scenario. Think about what Kwame is doing right and what he is doing wrong.

Consider it

Read these six tips for how to make the most of a dictionary. Discuss each one with a partner. Which ones do you do?

1 **Choose carefully** Not all dictionaries are the same. Decide which type would best serve your needs. For example, do you want a bilingual or English-only dictionary? There are specialist dictionaries to consider as well, such as learner's dictionaries, academic vocabulary dictionaries, and idioms dictionaries.

2 **Get familiar with your dictionary** The best way to familiarize yourself with a dictionary is to read the introduction. This explains how entries are arranged. It also contains useful information on the key abbreviations and pronunciation symbols used in the dictionary.

3 **Be efficient** Try to look up works quickly. Be familiar with alphabetical order and use the guidewords at the top of the page to save time. If you cannot find a word, do not give up. You may need to check other possible spellings of the word.

4 **Locate the correct definition** When you look up a new word, think about how the entries relate to the word. Look for the correct part of speech for the word and decide which definition is correct. The most common meaning is usually placed first.

5 **Study the entry in detail** Besides one or more definitions, a word's entry may include the pronunciation, example sentences, synonyms and antonyms, and other words derived from the same word.

6 **Use the dictionary for other things** You may also find photos and illustrations, maps, lists of famous people, lists of countries and their capitals, flags of countries, and weights and measurements tables.

Over to you

Discuss these questions with a partner.

1 Which of the tips do you follow?
2 How else can you find the meaning of new words?
3 What is one advantage and one disadvantage of electronic dictionaries?

Dictionary /ˈdɪkʃəˌneri/

NOUN [C]

a book that gives an alphabetical list of words with their meanings or their translations

Kwame has been studying English for two years. He uses a bilingual dictionary when he does his homework. He only uses a dictionary to look up words he does not understand. When he looks up a word, he uses the guidewords at the top of the pages to help him find the word quickly. He reads every definition until he finds the correct one. He does not usually check the pronunciation because he is not familiar with the symbols his dictionary uses. He likes to check the example sentences to make sure the definition he chose is the right one. Kwame keeps his dictionary in his study space, but he also keeps a smaller pocket dictionary in his book bag.

Work

READING	Sequencing
	Reading charts and
	graphs
VOCABULARY	Using collocations
WRITING	Using parallel
	structure
GRAMMAR	Future forms

Discussion point

Discuss these questions with a partner.

1   Look at the picture. Would you like to work there? Why or why not?

   I would love / hate to work there because ...

2   Do you enjoy hard work? Why or why not?

   I enjoy / don't enjoy hard work because ...

3   Choose one quotation. What does it mean to you? Put it your own words.

   To me, this quotation means ...

"If you cannot work with love but only with distaste, it is better that you should leave your work."
Khalil Gibran, poet   Source: *The Prophet* (1923)

"I learned the value of hard work by working hard."
Margaret Mead, anthropologist

"Whatever your life's work is, do it well."
Martin Luther King, Jr., civil rights leader

"I never did a day's work in my life. It was all fun."
Thomas A. Edison, inventor

Vocabulary preview

Cross out the words that do not have similar meanings to the words in bold.

1	**assess**	to reverse	to examine	to evaluate
2	**distant**	remote	close	faraway
3	**fortune**	money	appearance	wealth
4	**grateful**	thankful	appreciative	annoyed
5	**maintenance**	downgrade	preservation	repairs
6	**mundane**	ordinary	detailed	common
7	**precise**	exact	accurate	average
8	**repetitive**	easy	recurring	over and over

READING 1 The farmer's lazy son

Before you read

What folktales from your culture do you know? What are the morals of these stories? Discuss with a partner.

I know a folktale called ... . It's about ... . The moral is ...

Global reading

1 **Read the first paragraph of *The farmer's lazy son*. Check (✓) your prediction for what will happen in the next paragraph.**

   1 ☐ Someone will find a way to get Paolo to work.

   2 ☐ Marcos will find someone else to work in the fields.

2 **Now read the rest of the story. After each paragraph, stop and predict what will happen next. Were you able to predict much of the story?**

Close reading

SEQUENCING

When you sequence events you put them in the order in which they occur. Sequencing is useful for gaining a deeper understanding of the relationship between events. Most narrative stories are constructed around a series of events. Other text types can also be organized around a sequence, such as instructions, historical texts, and scientific observations.

---

1 **Number these key events in *The farmer's lazy son* in order.**

   a Marcos' friend Luigi stopped by one day. ___

   b Marcos told Paolo about a map. ___

   c Marcos dropped something into the dirt. ___

   d Paolo looked for the gold again the next day. ___

   e Paolo went back to his lazy ways. ___

   f Paolo worked hard and made his father proud. ___

   g Marcos worked all day while his lazy son Paulo did nothing. *1*

   h Paolo decided not to look for the gold anymore. ___

   i Paolo learned an important lesson. ___

   j Luigi told Marcos about his idea to get Paolo to work. ___

   k Marcos showed Paolo the treasure in the fields. ___

   l Paolo dug in the dirt looking for gold coins. ___

MORALS

appreciate what you have

be kind to others

do not judge

love your family

never steal or lie

respect your elders

share

work hard

2 Check (✓) the author's purpose. There are two answers.

1 ☐ inform   **2** ☐ entertain   **3** ☐ persuade

THE
FARMER'S LAZY SON

¹ Marcos was a farmer. He worked hard his whole life. Every day he asked his only son Paolo to help him in the fields, but Paolo rarely got out of bed before noon. He found farming mundane and repetitive. Marcos worked all day in the hot sun, but Paolo never helped. Marcos was very sad about his only son.

² One evening Marcos' old friend Luigi stopped by. "Marcos, why aren't your fields ready for planting? You won't have enough time to get your crop in!" Marcos explained that he was old, that his back hurt, and that he was tired. He said that Paolo was lazy and did not help with the farming or maintenance of the fields. "Marcos, you need to use your brain as much as your back. I have an idea for you." Luigi said.

³ Early the next morning Marcos rushed into Paolo's bedroom. "I found your grandfather's map!" he cried. "It's not very precise but I think we can find where he buried his gold coins!" Paolo jumped out of bed. "I'll start over here," Paolo told his father. Paolo dug in the field all morning. While Paolo dug, his father followed along, dropping something from his bag into the ground.

⁴ The next day they assessed the situation and decided that maybe they were in the wrong field, so they moved to another one. All day Paolo dug, looking for gold and again, his father stayed close behind. When they went in for dinner that night, a very tired Paolo said, "I think Grandfather was old when he made his map. I don't think I'll dig tomorrow. I think I'll go fishing with my friends instead."

⁵ Paolo returned to his lazy ways. He complained about his two days wasted in the fields. He spent the next month staying out late, sleeping until noon, and spending time at the river with his lazy friends.

⁶ One day Marcos rushed into Paolo's room and cried "Paolo! I found the treasure in the field!" Paolo sleepily went out to look. He said, "There is nothing here but rows and rows of vegetables."

⁷ Marcos smiled. "Paolo, it is all around you. You have enough food to make it through the winter, with plenty more to sell! You will make a small fortune at the market." Paolo was embarrassed to see that his father was right. His two days of hard work had provided him with real treasure. He learned an important lesson and he was very grateful. He could make a good living with a little hard work. He became a good farmer and made his father proud.

Developing critical thinking

Discuss these questions in a group.

1 What is the moral of the story?

The moral of the story is ...

2 What do you think Paolo learned?

I think Paolo learned ... . He shows this when he ...

3 Stories are often used to teach morals. How else can you learn morals?

There are many ways to learn morals, such as ...

ACADEMIC KEYWORDS

explain	(v)	/ɪkˈspleɪn/
follow	(v)	/ˈfɑloʊ/
situation	(n)	/ˌsɪtʃuˈeɪʃ(ə)n/

READING 2 Leave it for the robot

Before you read

What jobs do you think the robots in the pictures do? Discuss with a partner.

I think that robot ... because the picture shows ...

Global reading

1 **Skim *Leave it for the robot*. Write what the text is about.**

2 **Scan *Leave it for the robot*. Complete these sentences.**

   1 There are _____ of robots at work around the world.
   2 The most common type of robotic device is a _____.
   3 Two things ROVs can do are _____ and _____.
   4 The Roomba is a type of home robot that _____ floors.

Close reading

READING CHARTS AND GRAPHS

Texts sometimes contain charts and graphs, which show information in a
visual way. Charts and graphs often contain key information that is not
discussed in detail in a text. They are organized so you can read and
interpret the information quickly.

Pie charts show percentages

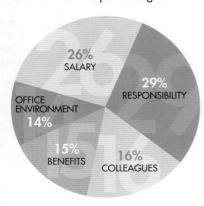

26% SALARY
29% RESPONSIBILITY
OFFICE ENVIRONMENT 14%
15% BENEFITS
16% COLLEAGUES

What people consider the most important
factor in a job

Bar graphs show comparisons
or changes.

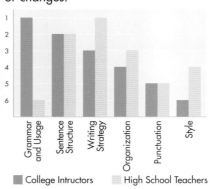

Grammar and Usage | Sentence Structure | Writing Strategy | Organization | Punctuation | Style

■ College Intructors   ■ High School Teachers

Most important writing skills as ranked by high
school and college teachers

1 **Read *Leave it for the robot*. Then look at Figure 1. Discuss these questions.**

   1 What country has a slightly lower robot density than the U.S.?
   2 What country has the highest robot density?
   3 What country is South Korea closest to in terms of robot density?

2 **Look at Figure 2. Write the answers to these questions.**

   1 What task would almost 70% of people like robots to do?
   2 What percentage of people would like robots to move heavy things?
   3 What task has about the same percentage of people who would and
      would not like robots to do it?

JOBS

clean   make things
investigate   shop

Leave it for THE ROBOT

[1] Dirty, dangerous, and dull. These are three words you do not want to describe your job. While many jobs are a little dirty, dangerous, or dull, some are so much so that it is better not to have humans performing them at all. Would you want to be the first person to go into a building with a fire? What if a robot could assess and fix the situation? This is already happening all around the world. There are millions of robots at work today. Japan leads the way, followed by Singapore, South Korea, and Germany (see Figure 1).

[2] The most common type of robotic device is a mechanical arm. This is often used in manufacturing. These arms move in many directions and perform precise and repetitive tasks with ease. But robots have moved well beyond such simple and mundane tasks. A robot named *Demeter* is an agricultural harvester that can move around a field of crops, planting and harvesting by using GPS, controllers, and sensors.

[3] Some robots are programmed to do certain jobs, but others are remotely operated vehicles (ROVs). ROVs can have cameras, sensors, and other devices that provide hard-to-obtain information. The U.S. space agency NASA has used ROVs to explore the surface of the moon and Mars. ROVs are also used in underwater environments. They can perform maintenance on oil drilling platforms and explore the ocean floors. They are also used to gather information on geographical changes in volcanoes.

[4] What do regular people want from robots? As seen in Figure 2, people would like robots to perform tasks around the house. One home robot on the market now is *Roomba*, a turtle-shaped robot that slowly vacuums its way around the room. It senses walls and turns to avoid stairs and objects on the floor. A robot that washes the windows and does the dishes could make someone a small fortune!

[5] Robots will play a more important role in the future. Surely they will continue to explore the ocean, analyze the surface of distant planets, and build our cars and computers. But what else? Will more robots drive our cars for us? Will they do our laundry? Will they do our gardening? Perhaps. When someone invents that window-cleaning robot, they will be rewarded by a grateful population.

Top ten countries by robot density
(Industial robots per 10,000 manufacturing workers)

JAPAN	295
SINGAPORE	169
SOUTH KOREA	164
GERMANY	163
SWEDEN	126
BELGIUM	89
U.S.	86
SPAIN	84

Figure 1

What should robots do?

- Vacuum cleaning
- Window cleaning
- Floor cleaning
- Moving heavy things
- Ironing
- Dusting
- Bathroom cleaning
- Laundry
- Dish washing
- Sports partner

0% 20% 40% 60% 80%

■ I would not like robots to do this
■ I would like robots to do this

Figure 2

ACADEMIC KEYWORDS

certain	(adj)	/ˈsɜrt(ə)n/
perform	(v)	/pərˈfɔrm/
role	(n)	/roʊl/

THINK ABOUT:

family	money
health	time
laziness	work

Developing critical thinking

1 Discuss these questions in a group.

1 What are some advantages and disadvantages of robots doing work for humans? Think about the things in the box on the right.

Advantages	Disadvantages
more time to spend with family	

2 What tasks do you think robots will and will not do in the future?

In the future, I think robots will … . I don't think they'll …

2 Think about the ideas from *The farmer's lazy son* and *Leave it for the robot* and discuss these questions in a group.

1 Do you think people are naturally lazy? Why or why not?

I think / don't think people are naturally lazy because …

2 Could robots make people lazier? Why or why not?

It's possible / impossible that robots could make people lazier because …

Vocabulary skill

USING COLLOCATIONS

A collocation is two or more words that naturally go together. For example, we say *fast food* but not *quick food*. Using collocations makes your writing sound more natural.

Study these tips for learning collocations:

- Read a lot to see and learn collocations in a natural context.
- Treat collocations as blocks of language, not individual words.
- Learn them in groups. (e.g. *take your time, take a break, take a nap*)
- When you learn a new word, write words that collocate with it. (e.g. new word = *utterly*, collocations = *utterly rude, utterly failed,* etc.)

1 In each set of four, match the words that collocate.

1	firm ___	**a** story	5	deep ___	**e** surprise
2	heavy ___	**b** handshake	6	strong ___	**f** energy
3	sore ___	**c** throat	7	big ___	**g** opinion
4	funny ___	**d** traffic	8	high ___	**h** pockets

2 Cross out the words that do not collocate with the words in bold.

1	**have**	lunch	an idea	a problem	the housework
2	**get**	a decision	permission	ready	lost
3	**do**	homework	the dishes	the laundry	a promise
4	**make**	an effort	thanks	a mistake	a noise
5	**go**	married	overseas	crazy	shopping
6	**pay**	attention	the bill	work	a visit
7	**take**	an exam	a shower	a taxi	sorry
8	**keep**	busy	an apology	a promise	calm
9	**find**	a break	the answer	the time	the way
10	**save**	time	money	a favor	energy

3 Complete these sentences. Use some of the collocations in exercise 2.

1 Can we have _____ soon? I'm getting really hungry.

2 Would you hurry up and get _____? We need to leave soon.

3 I need to do _____. All of my clothes are dirty.

4 Did you make _____ on my bill? I did not order any dessert.

5 You need to get a passport before you go _____.

6 I plan to pay _____ to my grandmother this weekend. I miss her.

7 There is no time to wait for the bus. We will take _____ instead.

8 If you ever find yourself in an emergency, it is important to keep _____.

9 Read the last paragraph carefully. You can find _____ there.

10 An easy way to save _____ is to shut down your computer at night.

WRITING Describing your future

You are going to learn about using parallel structure and using future forms. You are then going to use these to write a paragraph describing where you see yourself in five years.

Writing skill

▌USING PARALLEL STRUCTURE ▐

Parallel structures have the same patterns of words in a sentence to show that two or more ideas have equal importance. This can happen at the word, phrase, or clause level. The usual way to join parallel structures is with *and* or *or*.

*Tomorrow I think I'll **take** a long nap, **go** fishing, or **swim** in the river.*

*Paolo spent the next month **staying** out late, **sleeping** until noon, and **spending** time at the river with his lazy friends.*

These sentences do *not* have parallel structure:

*Tomorrow I think I'll take a long nap, go fishing, or **swimming** in the river.*

*Paolo spent the next month staying out late, sleeping until noon, and **spent** time at the river with his lazy friends.*

1 **Read these incorrect sentences about robots. Each has three structures that should be parallel. <u>Underline</u> them in each sentence.**

1 In 1939, a robot named *Elektro* was able to walk, count on its fingers and spoke words.

2 Most robots today are used to doing jobs that are repetitive, mundane, or danger.

3 Robots are also used in factories to build things like cars, appliances, and make electronics.

4 Some robots are designed to explore underwater, go down into volcanoes, and traveling to other planets.

5 Robots have been sent to Mars to collect soil, rock and atmosphere samples, analyze them, and then will send the data back to Earth.

6 Another reason we use robots is because they never get sick, take a day off, or complained!

7 Most robots usually have at least three main parts—the "brain" that is run by a computer program, mechanical parts that make the robot move, and sensors to tell the robot about its surroundings.

8 Unlike in TV programs, robots are unable to think, feel, or makes decisions.

2 **Now correct the sentences in exercise 1 to make them parallel in structure.**

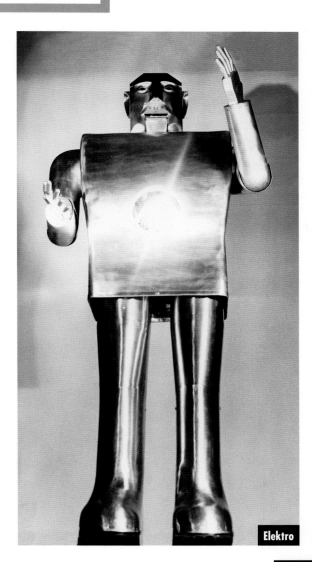

Elektro

Grammar

FUTURE FORMS

To form the simple future tense, use *will* + the base form of the verb.

Use the simple future tense in these situations …

1 To express a promise: *I will help you as soon as I finish breakfast.*

2 To make a prediction: *It will rain today.*

3 To state a spontaneous decision: *I will start over here.*

4 To state a possible future plan (with *think*): *I think I will go fishing.*

Study the forms:

Form	Example
Affirmative subject + *will* + base form	I will stay home today.
Negative subject + *will not (won't)* + base form	I will not stay home today.

1 Match the sentences with the situations.

1 I think I will go to Jordan on my vacation. ___   **a** To express a promise

2 I will call you as soon as I get home. ___   **b** To make a prediction

3 I want to watch TV. I will look for the remote. ___   **c** To state a spontaneous decision

4 Credit cards will never replace cash. ___   **d** To state a possible future plan

2 Complete these sentences. Use the simple future tense of the verbs in the box.

do	finish	look	not rain	quit	work

1 I _____ this report.

2 I promise I _____ harder.

3 I am sure it _____ this weekend.

4 John _____ his job tomorrow.

5 I do not think I _____ for a job right away.

6 I am sure you _____ well in your job interview.

3 Write four predictions about the future. Use these topics or your own ideas. Use the simple future tense. Then compare with a partner.

education	health	money
people	robots	technology	work

WRITING TASK

Read this paragraph. <u>Underline</u> the verbs in the simple future tense. There is one error in parallel structure. Correct it.

Bright future ahead

I think that my future will be very bright. I'm currently in my third year of college and next year I will be a senior. After I graduate, I will probably travel for a couple of weeks, see some friends, and then to look for a job. I'm studying to be an engineer so I would like to get a job in an engineering firm in my hometown. It won't be easy, but I will do my best. In three years I think I will try to buy a house. I want a house that is near my parents, that isn't too expensive, and that isn't far from work. I don't know, but I hope I will be married in four years. I'd like to start a family in about five years. I'm sure I will have a lot of children someday. That's what I think will happen, but of course no one can predict the future!

BRAINSTORM

Where do you see yourself in the next five years? Think about school, family, career, and other goals. Complete the timeline with years and details.

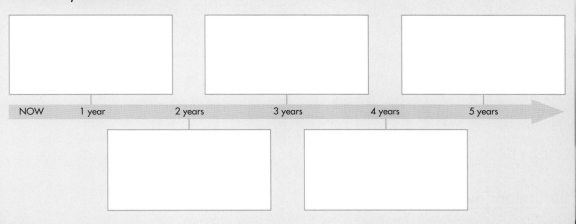

NOW   1 year   2 years   3 years   4 years   5 years

PLAN

Plan a paragraph describing where you see yourself in five years. Look back at your brainstorm and write a topic sentence. Decide how to organize your paragraph. Use at least two examples of parallel structure.

WRITE

Write your paragraph. Pay attention to your use of the simple future tense. Check any collocations in a dictionary.

SHARE

Exchange paragraphs with a partner. Look at the checklist on page 109 and provide feedback to your partner.

REWRITE AND EDIT

Consider your partner's comments and rewrite your paragraph.

Making the most of the library

by Stella Cottrell

Library services

The starting place for most research is the library. Join your local library, and find out about the services available.

Typically, there will be:

- academic journals
- specialist collections
- photocopiers
- laminators
- binding facilities
- computers
- CDs, DVDs, films, tapes, slides, and video resources
- silent areas and study rooms
- specialist resources for students with disabilities
- facilities for making audiovisual aids for your presentations
- support on how to use library facilities.

Catalogues

Most catalogues are now electronic. There may also be specialist collections for your subject, as well as indexes for national collections. It is quite usual to need help using these – if you are uncertain, don't be afraid to ask.

Make the library our own

Walk around the library and become familiar with the atmosphere. Sit at different tables and try different rooms. Where would you work best?

To see how the library works, look up books from your reading list. Try out the technology. It is designed to be easy to use even if you know nothing about computers – have a go!

You did say to make myself at home in the library

Find out basic information

- How many items can you take out at once?
- How many items can you take home on loan?
- How long does it take for books to come from the store, or from other sites?
- For how long can you have books out?
- Can you reserve books?
- Can you reserve or renew by telephone or the Internet?
- Are there fines?
- How do you make inter-library loans?
- Are there subject-specialist librarians?

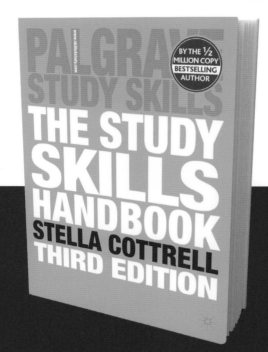
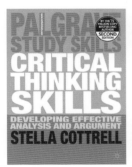

The phrases below give common ways of expressing useful functions. Use them to help you as you're completing the *Discussion points* and *Developing critical thinking* activities.

Asking for clarification

Sorry, can you explain that some more?
Could you say that another way?
When you say … do you mean …?
Sorry, I don't follow that.
What do you mean?

Asking for repetition

Could you repeat that, please?
I'm sorry, I didn't catch that.
Could you say that again?

When you don't know the word for something

What does … mean?
Sorry, I'm not sure what … means.

Working with a partner

Would you like to start?
Shall I go first?
Shall we do this one first?
Where do you want to begin?

Giving opinions

I think that …
It seems to me that …
In my opinion …
As I see it …

Agreeing and disagreeing

I know what you mean.
That's true.
You have a point there.
Yes. I see what you're saying, but …
I understand your point, but …
I don't think that's true.

Asking for opinions

Do you think …
Do you feel …
What do you think about …?
How about you, Jennifer? What do you think?
What about you?
Does anyone have any other ideas?
Do you have any thoughts on this?

Asking for more information

In what way?
Why do you think that?
Can you give an example?

Not giving a strong preference

It doesn't matter to me.
I don't really have a strong preference.
I've never really thought about that.
Either is fine.

Expressing interest

I'd like to hear more about that.
That sounds interesting.
How interesting!
Tell me more about that.

Giving reasons

This is … because …
This has to be … because …
I think … because …

Checking understanding

Do you know what I mean?
Do you see what I'm saying?
Are you following me?

Putting things in order

This needs to come first because …
I think this is the most / least important because …
For me, this is the most / least relevant because …

Writing task peer review checklist

Use the checklist below as you read over your partner's work.

PROCESS WRITING CHECKLIST

1 Does the paragraph have these things:

name ☐
class ☐
the date ☐
a title ☐

2 Could you follow the main idea of the paragraph? Is it a good response to the writing assignment?

3 Does every sentence begin and end with correct punctuation? Is every paragraph indented?

4 What is your favorite sentence or point from the paragraph?

5 Did you notice any target vocabulary from the unit? Write it here:

_____

6 Highlight any target grammar from the unit.

7 Underline the topic sentence or sentences.

8 Write one question about the paragraph for the writer.

Reviewers (sidebar)

The publishers would like to thank the following for their thoughtful insights and perceptive comments during the development of the material:

Belgium

Sylviane Granger, at CECL, University of Louvain
Magali Paquot

Egypt

Dr Gaber Khalil, AUC, Cairo

Germany

John Nixon at Universität Stuttgart

Japan

Robert Morton at Chuo University
Lesley Burda Ito

Oman

Mutaz Abumuaath at Nizwa College of Technology, Nizwa

Qatar

Jane Hoelker at Qatar University, Foundation English

Saudi Arabia

Dr Mohammed Hamdan, Imam Muhammad Ibn Saud University
Mohammed AL-Ahaydib, Imam University
William Frawley, Education Experts
Heidi Omara

South Korea

Yoonji Kim, and Da young Song at the Konkuk University Language Institute
Jina Kwon at Seoul National University

Taiwan

Laura Wang at Chung Yuan Christian University
Regina Jan at Lunghwa University of Science and Technology
Kitty Chu, Jessie Huang, Jenny Jen, and Wenyau Keng at the National Central University, Language Center
Sandrine Ting at the Department of Applied Foreign Language, St. John's University

Thailand

Sureepan Thepud, Nattinee Khueansri, Nongluck Srivichai, and Penporn Jatuworapruk at Payap University
Wanpen Chaikitmongkol, Jindarat De Vleeschauwer, and Sonhsi Wichaidit at the English Division, Department of Western Languages and Humanities, Chiang Mai University

Turkey

Merve Oflaz at Bahcesehir University
Şahika Özkan-Tuğba Kın-Yadigar Aslan, Didem Gümüşlüoğlu, Meltem Sarandal, and Sibel Weeks at Doğuş University, İstanbul
Sevil Altikulaçoğlu, Sühendan Semine Er, Şerife Ersöz, Fatma Ünveren Gürocak at Gazi University
Deniz Ateşok at Istanbul Bilgi University
Ebru Yamaç at Maltepe University,
Aybike Oğuz at Özyeğin University

United Arab Emirates

Paul Barney, Doug Henderson, and Danielle Norris at Higher Colleges of Technology, Al Ain

United Kingdom

Nick Hillman at Anglia Ruskin University
Heather Abel and Richard Hillman at Bell London
Edward Bressan, Sara Hanam, and Stacey Hughes at Oxford Brookes University
Fiodhna Gardiner-Hyland at University of Limerick
Sally Morris, Ian Pople, and Simon Raw at University of Manchester
Jonathan Hadley

United States

Gail Schafers at Fontbonne Univeristy
Carole Mawson at Stanford University
Denise Mussman at University of Missouri
Abby Brown

Macmillan Education
Between Towns Road, Oxford OX4 3PP
A division of Macmillan Publishers Limited
Companies and representatives throughout the world

ISBN 978-0-230-42975-8

Text, design and illustration © Macmillan Publishers Limited 2012
Written by David Bohlke
Series Consultant Dorothy E. Zemach

First published 2012

Designed by eMC Design Ltd
Illustrated by eMC Design Ltd
Cover design by eMC Design Ltd
Cover photograph by Thinkstock/iStockphoto
Picture research by Emily Taylor

The Academic Keyword List (AKL) was developed by Magali Paquot
within the framework of a research project led by Professor Sylviane
Granger at the Centre for English Corpus Linguistics, Université
catholique de Louvain, Belgium.
http://www.uclouvain.be/en-372126.html

Authors' acknowledgements

As a materials writer I am indebted to the many professionals I have
worked with over the years. I am especially grateful to the following
for their professional mentoring and the high standards they have
instilled in me: Jack C. Richards, Mary Vaughn, Deborah Goldblatt,
Jeff Krum, Amy McCormick, Arlen Gargagliano, Donna Brinton, and
Tom Wharton.

I would also like to sincerely thank series consultant Dorothy Zemach,
as well as the entire Macmillan Education team for their ongoing
guidance, support, and patience through the development of this
course.

The Author and Publishers would like to thank the following for
permission to reproduce their images:

ACT Communications – (http://www.act.org/activity/winter2004/
images/graph1.jpg) p100(bar chart);
Alamy/Bullysoft p17, Alamy/David Burton p94, Alamy/DWC p89(cl),
Alamy/Tor Eigeland p61(cm), Alamy/Joe Fox p14, Alamy/Ikon Images
p31, Alamy/Purepix p99(bm), Alamy/Peter Scholey p30(br), Alamy/
Rodger Tamblyn p52, Alamy/UwesMASAIMARA p37, Alamy/View
Pictures Ltd p51(tm), Alamy/Weidman Photography p67, Alamy/
www.white-windmill.co.uk p50(tr);
Apple Inc/Courtesy of Apple Inc p86;
Ardea/Doc White p39;
Corbis pp38(tr), 58, Corbis/Alan Schein Photography p34, Corbis/
Mike Agliolo p19, Corbis/Amana Images p40, Corbis/Bettman
Archive p103, Corbis/Charcrit Boonsom p43, Corbis/Xiao chun p97,
Corbis/Paul Cox p66, Corbis/Wolfgang Deuter p57, Corbis/DLILLC
p9, Corbis/DPA p8(cl), Corbis/Franck Guiziou p80(cr), Corbis/Billy
Hustace p93, Corbis/Image Source pp25, 70(2), Corbis/Adam Jones
p20, Corbis/Mike Kemp/Rubberball p46, Corbis/Mike Kowalski
p61(cr), Corbis/Beau Lark p88(tr), Corbis/Gideon Mendel p100(cr),
Corbis/Ocean p11, 49, 70(6), Corbis/Pulse p50(br), Corbis/Ron
Royals p30(tr), Corbis/Sagel & Kranefeld pp30(cr), 54, Corbis/Hugh
Sitton p28(tr), Corbis/Tom Stewart p48, Corbis/Tetra Images pp15,
70(3), Corbis/Topic Photo Agency p73, Corbis/David Wrobel p38(cr);
EPFL/ETHZ - Ray, C., Mondada, F. and Siegwart, R. (2008) What
do people expect from robots? Proceedings of the IEEE/RSJ 2008
International Conference on Intelligent Robots and Systems, pp.
3816-3821 p101(figure 2);
Getty Images pp8(bl), 70(1), Getty Images/Anne Ackermann
p88(br), Getty Images/AFP pp80(tr), 100(tr), Getty Images/AFP/
Prakash Mathema p81(tr), Getty Images/Agefotostock pp71(cr),
105, Getty Images/AsiaPac p78(br), Getty Images/AWL Images
p29, Getty Images/Gary S Chapman p12, Getty Images/Comstock
pp59(cr), 70(4), Getty Images/Alan Copson p55, Getty Images/
Dwight Eschliman p59(tm), Getty Images/George Frey p91, Getty
Images/Fry Design Ltd p35, Getty Images/G.K. & Vikki Hart p51(br),
Getty Images/Hulton Archive p8(cl), Getty Images/Hussain Shah
Photography p82, Getty/Image Bank Films p6(bl), Getty Images/
Image Source p36, Getty Images/Evgeniy Ivanov p96, Getty Images/
Ivary p21, Getty Images/Saul Landell p50(cr), Getty Images/Andy
Leong p63, Getty Images/Neil Massey p44, Getty Images/David
McGlynn p7, Getty Images/Ryan McVay pp24, 87, Getty Images/
Ulrich Mueller p47, Getty Images/Ian O'Leary p65, Getty Images/
Panoramic Images p71(tm), Getty Images/Corey Ralston p85, Getty
Images/Nicholas Rigg p16, Getty Images/Robert Harding World
Imagery pp28(br), 89(cr), Getty Images/Chris Sattlberger p99(cr),
Getty Images/Stockbyte p70(5), Getty Images/Stocktrek p100(br),
Getty Images/Time Life pp8(tl), 78(tr), Getty Images/Vetta p104,
Getty Images/Andrew Watson p27, Getty Images/Frank Whitney p95,
Getty Images/Yagi Studio p75;
IEEE Spectrum p101(figure 1);
Shaee Ilyas p70(tr);
Beau Lotto/Lottolab, p69(1), (2), (3), (4);
JP Masclet p8(br);
Photodisc p41;
Photoshot/Phil Degginger p77;
Picturenet p45;
Rex Features/Sipa p8(tr).

The author and publishers are grateful for permission to reprint the
following copyright material

Material from 'The Study Skills Handbook' by author Stella Cottrell,
copyright © Stella Cottrell 1999, 2003 & 2008, first published by
Palgrave Macmillan, reproduced with permission of the publisher.

Printed and bound in Thailand

2016 2015 2014 2013 2012
10 9 8 7 6 5 4 3 2 1

Recommended minimum system requirements for the *Skillful* Digibook

Windows

	Windows XP SP3	Vista	Windows 7
CPU Speed	Core 2 Duo, 2.53 GHz	Core 2 Duo, 2.53 GHz	Core 2 Duo, 2.93 GHz
Browser	Explorer 7, 8 & 9, Firefox, and Chrome		

Macintosh OS

	10.5	10.6	10.7
CPU Speed	Core 2 Duo – 1.83 GHz	Core 2 Duo – 1.83 GHz	Core 2 Duo – 1.83 GHz
Browser	Firefox and Safari 4 & 5		

Additional recommended minimum system requirements

- Hard Disk (offline version only): Minimum 1 GB free on the install drive and minimum 2 GB free on the system drive.
- Free RAM: 500 MB
- Display: 1024 x 768 pixels, 32-bit colour
- Add-ins: Flash Player 10.1
- Broadband connection: For Authentication/Registration/Download (offline version only)/Updates

Please visit help.macmillan.com for technical support

This software is licensed for use by one user and can be installed on a maximum of one machine.

Product Activation

1 Type *www.skillfuldigibooks.com* into your Internet browser.

2 Click "Enter your token details"

3 You need your access token code, printed on the next page.

4 Type your access token code into the box provided.

5 Follow the step-by-step instructions on the screen to help you register and log-in.

6 You can now use your *Skillful* DigiBook.

Your access token code only allows one user to log in, so don't give yours away, and make sure you use it within one year!